PROTECTING HATE SPEECH

R.A.V. V. ST. PAUL

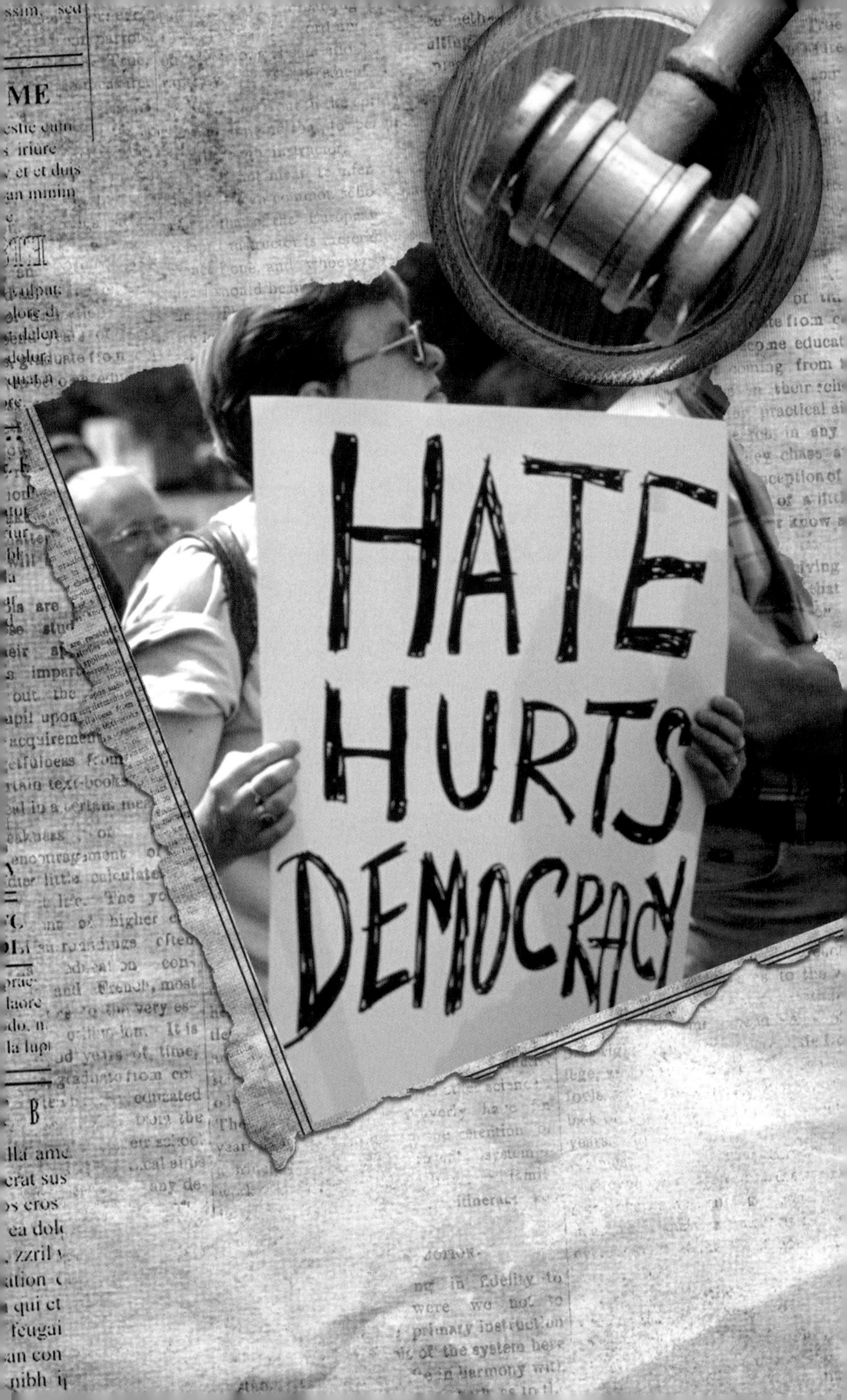
HATE
HURTS
DEMOCRACY

★★★ PRIC

FIRST AMENDMENT CASES

PROTECTING HATE SPEECH

R.A.V. V. ST. PAUL

By Susan Dudley Gold

Cavendish
Square

New York

With special thanks to David M. O'Brien, Spicer Professor, Department of Politics, University of Virginia, for his expert review of this manuscript.

CPSIA Compliance Information:
Batch #WW14CSQ

All websites were available and accurate when this book was sent to press.

LIBRARY OF CONGRESS
CATALOGING-IN-PUBLICATION DATA

Gold, Susan Dudley, author. Protecting hate speech : R.A.V. v. St. Paul / Susan Dudley Gold.
pages cm. — (First Amendment cases). Includes bibliographical references and index.
ISBN 978-1-62712-393-8 (hardcover)
ISBN 978-1-62712-394-5 (paperback)
ISBN 978-1-62712-395-2 (ebook)
1. R. A. V. (Robert A. Viktora)—Trials, litigation, etc.—Juvenile literature. 2. Saint Paul (Minn.)—Trials, litigation, etc.—Juvenile literature. 3. Trials (Hate crimes)—United States.—Juvenile literature. 4. Trials (Hate crimes)—Minnesota.—Juvenile literature. 5. Hate speech—Minnesota.—Juvenile literature. 6. Freedom of speech—United States—Juvenile literature. I. Title. KF224.R345G65 2014 342.7308'53—dc23
2013033264

Art Director: Anahid Hamparian
Series Designer: Michael Nelson
Photo Research: Custom Communications, Inc.

The photographs in this book are used by permission and through the courtesy of: Newscom: EPA/Jim Lo Scalzo, cover; Globe Photos/ZUMA PRESS.com, 97. Alamy: CLEO Photo, 2. Associated Press: 8, 65; Frankie Ziths, 14; David Cantor, 29; Don Ryan, 51; Barry Thumma, 66; Marcy Nighswander, 70; Pat Sullivan, 87; Mark R. Sullivan, 109; George Widman, 114; Ross D. Franklin, 117. Getty Images: Time & Life Pictures, 17, 19, 54, 59; 49; Abbott Sengstacke Family Papers, 24; AFP, 106. Minnesota Judicial Branch: 33, 57. Tom Foley: 42.

CONTENTS

FIRST AMENDMENT

THE FIRST AMENDMENT

Congress shall make no law respecting an establishment of religion, or prohibiting the free exercise thereof; or abridging the freedom of speech, or of the press; or the right of the people peaceably to assemble, and to petition the Government for a redress of grievances.

—*U.S. Constitution, Amendment I*

Hate Crimes

ON THE EVENING OF JUNE 18, 1984, A MEMBER OF a white supremacist group called The Order gunned down Alan Berg, a Jewish radio talk-show host, as he carried a bag of groceries from his car to his Denver townhouse. Berg, known for his irreverent, in-your-face style, had frequently mocked white supremacist groups during his radio broadcasts. This angered members of The Order, an anti-Semitic splinter group of the Aryan Nations. The Aryan Nations, founded in 1973 by Richard Butler, served as the center of the white supremacist movement in the United States. The Order's assassin pumped thirteen bullets from a MAC-10 submachine gun into Berg, who died instantly. He was fifty years old. Two of those charged in Berg's death were cleared of complicity in the murder but went to prison on unrelated criminal charges. Two others, including the suspected triggerman, were convicted of violating Berg's civil rights; they received lengthy prison sentences. The leader of the group, Robert Jay Mathews, later died in a fire during a police stakeout.

Talk radio icon Alan Berg expresses his views on air at a Denver station in 1978. A group of white separatists assassinated him six years later because they disagreed with his opinions.

The Order believed "in killing all the Jews and sending all the blacks back to Africa," said Anath White, who produced Berg's radio show in the 1980s. Berg was one of several Jews whose name appeared on a hit list compiled by the group. At the trial, federal Judge Richard Matsch said Berg "was killed for who he was, what he believed in, and what he said and did, and that crime strikes at the very core of the Constitution."

Berg's murder and several other incidents involving violence against victims targeted because of their race or religion spurred Congress to consider a bill dubbed the "Hate Crimes Statistics Act" in 1985. The term "hate crime" soon gained popularity in the media and legal circles, but the bill itself, which called for law enforcement officials to collect data on crimes involving bias, was not enacted until 1990.

Starting in the 1980s states and municipalities began passing hate-crime laws to punish those who targeted others because of their race, religion, or national origin. A few regulations also included crimes motivated by bias against a person's disability, sexual orientation, or gender. Some laws banned hate crimes outright. Others increased the penalties for criminals convicted of crimes involving bias. During the same period, colleges began adopting hate-speech codes that punished the use of biased language on campus.

As soon as these laws and codes began to appear, free-speech advocates questioned their broad reach. Critics of the laws argue that they penalize speech that is in fact protected by the First Amendment. They contend that such laws can prohibit speech or expression that is merely offensive or that one or more groups have judged to be "politically incorrect" or inappropriate. Opponents also assert that bias laws are not necessary or effective. They argue that laws already on the books are sufficient to punish criminals, that all crimes are "hateful," and that the law should treat crimes equally, regardless of whether bias is involved. "If the skulls of all Americans are equally valuable (i.e., if this is a democracy), why not give everyone [the same sentence] for cracking any cranium at all?" commentator John Leo asked in an article that appeared in *U.S. News & World Report* in 1989.

Proponents of the regulations contend that hate crimes that target groups such as African Americans and Jews, who have been the victims of massive injustice in the past, cause more damage than mere insults or a crime not motivated by bias. Words reflecting hate and actions motivated by bias, those who favor regulation say, cause increased emotional and psychological harm to people already victimized by society. The harm can spread as other members of the group begin to feel intimidated. Hate-motivated activities harm the community, too, when they cause minorities to feel fearful and separated from the rest of the population. Hate-crime laws are necessary, many believe, to emphasize the community's support of members of groups targeted by bigots and to take a stand against discrimination and prejudice.

HATE SPEECH AND THE FIRST AMENDMENT

Despite its strong guarantees of free speech, the First Amendment as interpreted by the U.S. Supreme Court does not protect all types of speech. Court rulings have allowed certain restrictions on speech and expressive acts, among them utterances that incite imminent violence ("fighting words"), libel or slander of a person or organization, true threats, words that pose a "clear and present danger" to the government, and obscene material with no artistic or other redeeming value.

Many Americans believe that hate speech should be among the forms of utterances not protected by the Constitution. But on June 22, 1992, the Supreme Court ruled differently. In a unanimous decision, the Court for the first time decreed that hate speech falls under the protection of the First Amendment. The ruling, in *R.A.V. v. St. Paul*, invalidated many hate-crime and hate-speech regulations across the nation. The incident that led to the ruling—the burning of a cross in a black family's yard in St. Paul, Minnesota—ignited the community's outrage, a response that spread across the country as the case gained notoriety. Almost everyone involved, from the lawyers of the teenage defendant to the prosecutor to the U.S. Supreme Court justices, agreed that the act of cross burning was reprehensible and ought to be punished. The controversy arose because officials in St. Paul had chosen to base prosecution on a city ordinance targeted at hate crimes.

Although all nine justices voted against the city, they split 5-to-4 when giving their reasons for striking the ordinance. Five members supported Justice Antonin Scalia's majority decision, which seemed to strike a blow against all laws that differentiated between speech and crimes motivated by hate and those not bias related. Scalia argued that such laws violated the First

Amendment because they allowed officials to mete out punishment based on the views held by offenders. Four other justices made the case that the St. Paul law criminalized too much speech that merited First Amendment protection, including words that were merely offensive. The minority opinion opened the door to hate-crime regulations that more narrowly targeted expressions and acts that did not qualify for protection under the First Amendment. A year later, in *Wisconsin v. Mitchell*, the Court—again unanimously—expanded its position on hate-crime laws by upholding a state law that increased penalties for crimes motivated by bigotry. The ruling allowed a defendant's biased words to be considered during the sentencing phase in order to establish motive. According to the Court, the Wisconsin law, unlike the St. Paul ordinance, focused on a defendant's conduct (criminal behavior) and took into account his bigoted ideas only as a factor in his sentence. The decision did not overturn the *R.A.V.* ruling.

Some critics believe the Supreme Court should not have barred laws such as St. Paul's, which target bias-motivated speech and acts. Others believe the Court got it right in the *R.A.V. v. St. Paul* decision but erred in the ruling on *Mitchell*.

So far, the courts have ruled against college hate-speech codes in every case that has come before them. Many of the codes, however, remain in place, either unchallenged in court or buried within rules of behavior. For the most part, lower courts have followed the Supreme Court's lead and upheld federal, state, and local statutes that increase penalties for bias-motivated crimes.

Questions still remain over hate-crime laws. Is the murder of someone whose fancy car attracted the killer any less heinous than the murder of someone whose religion incensed the murderer? Are hate-crime laws effective in reducing bigotry and prejudice? Do they give officials too much power in determining whether a person's views qualify as hate speech? Do they protect members of minority groups? Or do they jeopardize people's right to express views held by a minority of Americans?

Hate crimes disgust almost everyone. Gruesome, cold-blooded acts such as the murder of Alan Berg have produced an outcry among Americans demanding that steps be taken to prevent hate crimes. Perpetrators of these unthinkable acts must indeed be punished to the full extent of the law. The Supreme Court has made clear, however, by its rulings in *R.A.V.* and other cases, that officials cannot infringe on Americans' right to free speech, even when it means that hate-spewing, vicious utterances will go unpunished.

During the 1980s U.S. news organizations reported a growing number of hate crimes—those motivated by bias against a victim's race, religion, or other characteristic. The shooting death of a black teen, Yusef Hawkins, by a mob of white hoodlums in Brooklyn, New York, in 1989 stirred up racial tension in the neighborhood and raised concerns over hate crimes in general. Here, a crowd heckles marchers protesting Hawkins's killing.

CHAPTER ONE

A CRIME AGAINST PEOPLE

AT 2:30 ON THE MORNING OF JUNE 21, 1990, Russell and Laura Jones looked out the window of their house to see a group of neighborhood teens burning a two-foot cross in their yard. Before dawn, the group of boys had burned two other crosses—crudely made from chair legs tied together—near the Joneses' home in the working-class east side of St. Paul, Minnesota. The Joneses, a black couple with five children, had moved to the formerly all-white community three months before the incident. They called the police department to report what they considered to be a threat.

The cross burning marked the first time in decades that anyone had witnessed such a spectacle in the city. Officials said, however, that acts of terrorism against nonwhites were on the rise. Fifteen of the thirty such incidents in St. Paul in the first six months of 1990 occurred on the east side of the city, where the Joneses lived, police reported. The harassment reports followed an increase in the number of African Americans and members of other racial minorities moving into the area.

It was not the first time the Jones family had been harassed. Someone had smashed the tailgate window on their station wagon and slashed the tires. Local teenagers had hurled racial slurs at the Jones children. Laura Jones told reporters she would not be run off, but her husband expressed concern for the family's safety. "I wonder how long it will be before they start attacking the house," he said. "I'm concerned about the kids going outside to play."

Police had already connected a group of skinheads with other racial incidents in the area. Skinheads, young white men who shaved their heads and espoused violence against nonwhites, had been implicated in the beating and robbery of a young African American boy, in the harassment of an interracial couple, and in the beating of an African American man with a stick, after which the skinheads ordered a dog to attack their victim. "The Police Department is vehemently opposed to this behavior . . . and will vigorously investigate it and prosecute it," deputy police chief Ted Brown told reporters.

Several days later, police arrested two white teenage

Russell Jones (*left*) and his wife, Laura, get their five children ready for church in December 1991.

boys and charged them with violating a city ordinance that made it a crime to burn a cross or commit a similar act that would create "anger, alarm or resentment in others on the basis of race, color, creed, religion, or gender." The teens could have been charged with "terroristic threats," a felony that carried a sentence of up to three years in prison, police said.

Eighteen-year-old Arthur M. Miller III, the older youth, lived across the street from the Joneses. He eventually pleaded guilty to the misdemeanor charge and received a thirty-day jail sentence. The other youth, seventeen-year-old Robert A. Viktora, denied he had been involved in the cross burning. An anonymous caller tipped off police, reporting that Viktora had bragged to friends that he had burned the crosses. The teen, who was living in the Miller home at the time of the incident, could not afford to pay for a lawyer to represent him. Court officials turned the case over to Edward J. Cleary, a local attorney who worked part-time in the Ramsey County Public Defender's Office. Since Viktora was a minor when the case first came to court, he was referred to only by his initials, R.A.V., in the court's proceedings, as is usually done when the defendant is not being charged as an adult.

Cleary, a Minnesota-born Democrat who had represented many African American clients in his work, had not asked for the case. He had merely been the lawyer slated to take the next case for the public defender's office when Viktora, a juvenile without funds, sought representation. As the case gained national attention, Cleary and Michael Cromett, another public defender who served as cocounsel on the case, became the objects of media scrutiny. Criticized for supporting hate speech and cross burning, Cleary lost clients and received threats against his life and his family.

No one had ever been charged under St. Paul's anti-bias ordinance before. Enacted in 1982, the hate-crimes ordinance applied to acts that were motivated by bias based on "race, color, creed, or religion." The Bias-Motivated Crime Ordinance was amended in 1990 to add "gender" to the list of biases in the original law.

Attorney Edward Cleary preparing for the case against client Robert A. Viktora.

The regulation specifically prohibited anyone from placing on public or private property a burning cross, a Nazi swastika, or other object that symbolized bigotry. Although charged with a misdemeanor, criminals prosecuted under the law faced up to one year in jail. City councilors passed the legislation to help curb hate crimes, which they believed had been increasing in the region. "The city wanted to send a message that we wouldn't tolerate crimes against people because of their race or religion," said Mayor Jim Scheibel. He was council president when the ordinance was passed. The cross burning at the Joneses' house, Mayor Scheibel told reporters, was "not free speech. [It was] a crime against people."

ST. PAUL CITY ORDINANCE SECTION 292.02

Whoever places on public or private property a symbol, object, appellation, characterization or graffiti, including, but not limited to, a burning cross or Nazi swastika, which one knows or has reasonable grounds to know arouses anger, alarm or resentment in others on the basis of race, color, creed, religion or gender commits disorderly conduct and shall be guilty of a misdemeanor.

A "RASH" OF HATE CRIMES

A front-page story in the *Boston Globe* in July 1990 reported a "rash" of hate crimes across America and predicted that it would be the worst year yet for violent acts "motivated by race, religion and sexual preference." According to a survey conducted by the Massachusetts newspaper, New York City had 349 hate crimes in the first half of 1990, an increase of 29 percent from the previous year. Similar reports came from the cities of Chicago, Denver, and Boston, and in two states, Maryland and Minnesota.

The *Globe* article detailed several incidents of vicious attacks targeting gays and minorities. One involved a gay black man from Kentucky, who suffered severe brain damage after being beaten with a tire iron and locked in a car trunk with a snapping turtle. "Hate crime assault victims are three times more likely to need hospital attention than other assault victims," Jack McDevitt, a Northeastern University analyst studying hate crimes in Boston, told reporters.

Others in the field said hate crimes poisoned whole communities. "There is no other crime that destroys a person's dignity, their family, their community this way," said Detective Sergeant William Johnston of Boston Police Department's Community Disorders Unit. "These hate crimes are the worst."

In June 1990 the National Gay and Lesbian Task Force released the results of a survey of violence against gays in the United States. The survey reported around seven thousand incidents in 1989, ranging from verbal abuse to homicide—about two hundred fewer than the previous year. The Anti-Defamation League of B'nai B'rith, a Jewish organization, also released figures on bias-motivated acts. The organization's report showed bigotry against Jews had increased over previous years, with a total of 1,432 incidents in the country during 1989. Both groups found hope in the growing number of hate-crime laws in cities and states.

HATE–CRIME LAWS

Hate-crime laws became popular beginning in the 1980s as a way to curtail racially motivated violence. A number of colleges adopted speech codes barring language that derided a person's race, religion, or gender. Similarly, states and municipalities passed laws designed to punish hate crimes, which are offenses based on the victim's color, creed, or gender. In April 1990 President George H. W. Bush signed the Hate Crimes Statistics Act, which required the federal government to compile figures on hate crimes nationally. The legislation encompassed crimes motivated by "race, religion, sexual orientation, or ethnicity."

"Hate crimes exist because the narrow-minded and mean-spirited among us have judged some of their fellow citizens to be less deserving of respect than themselves," said Democratic senator Alan Cranston. "The more that we bring these crimes to light, the less tolerable they will be."

Advocates of the laws maintained that because hate speech evokes a long history of abuse, degradation, and humiliation, it is far more harmful than expression that is simply hostile. A burning cross would be exceptionally frightening for an African American because the symbol would bring to mind the lynchings and savage beatings black Americans endured at the hands of Ku Klux Klan members and others dedicated to white supremacy. An African American may have even witnessed the injury or death of a relative or friend under such circumstances. A white person, on the other hand, might be disturbed by a burning cross, but the sight would not hold the same level of terror as for a black man or woman. Similarly, advocates of the hate-crime laws believed that a person whose family had died in a Nazi concentration camp would suffer far more from the display of a swastika than someone who found the symbol offensive but who had had no connection to the Nazis.

Most of the hate-crime laws in place in 1990 merely increased the penalty given to offenders convicted of a crime involving bias. Defendants found guilty of arson, for example, received sentences that doubled the number of years in prison if their acts targeted victims based on race, religion, or other specified bias. St. Paul's ordinance differed from many hate-crime laws in that it made hate speech or conduct a separate crime, not just an aggravating factor that increased a convict's sentence. Neither type of hate-crime law had yet been tested in the Supreme Court. The cross burning at the Joneses' home would be the incident that triggered the high court's first hearing on hate crimes.

CHAPTER TWO

FREE SPEECH OR "FIGHTING WORDS"?

ROBERT A. VIKTORA, CHARGED WITH VIO-
lating St. Paul's hate-crime ordinance in connection
with the cross burning, pleaded not guilty to the
offense. Edward Cleary, the teen's public defender,
challenged the constitutionality of the law, claiming
it violated the right to free speech guaranteed by the
First Amendment. Officials set a hearing for the case
in Ramsey County District Court on July 13, 1990.

During the hearing, Cleary argued that the St. Paul
ordinance was too broad; in other words, it applied to
a wide range of actions, including some that should
not be considered illegal. Even if justified in a case
such as Viktora's, Cleary contended, the ordinance
could not be allowed to stay on the books because
it threatened legitimate expression protected by the

First Amendment. Even if the law was rarely invoked, its existence gave local officials a weapon to use against expression they found objectionable.

In a case decided in 1940, the U.S. Supreme Court established the standard for determining whether a law was too broad. That case, *Thornhill v. Alabama*, stemmed from the arrest of a union member named Byron Thornhill, who had asked a replacement worker not to cross a picket line during a strike. The company involved in the labor dispute complained that Thornhill, the union president, had interfered with its business by joining the picket line. Officials charged him under a state law that prohibited picketing in front of businesses.

In an 8-to-1 ruling, the Court struck down the Alabama law. The statute, the Court said, went far beyond punishing picketers who interfered with business. It also barred employees from talking about the facts involved in a labor dispute and from circulating pamphlets, signs, or other materials discussing the issues at hand. "The freedom of speech and of the press guaranteed by the Constitution embraces at least the liberty to discuss publicly and truthfully all matters of public concern, without previous restraint or fear of subsequent punishment," Justice Frank Murphy wrote in his majority opinion. Justice Murphy said that even if Thornhill's behavior could be punished under the Constitution, the law under which officials charged him was flawed. Because of that, the law had to be overturned and the charges against Thornhill dismissed. Decades later, the Court in *Brockett v. Sokane Arcades Inc.* (1985) made it more difficult to challenge overbroad laws by ruling that defendants had to prove that such statutes applied to a "substantial" quantity of speech protected under the Constitution. Nevertheless, the Court continued to strike down laws that were unconstitutionally broad.

If a law is unconstitutional, no one can be legally charged under it, even if the acts in question are not protected by the Constitution because they comprise criminal behavior. In St. Paul's case, while the hate-crime law might legitimately apply to the cross burning in the Joneses' yard, it also could have led to the arrest of a protester who distributed antigay pamphlets during a rally supporting same-sex marriage. The pamphlet, motivated by bias against homosexuals, would certainly arouse anger or resentment among the rally participants, but the First Amendment protects such material as an expression of a political viewpoint. The St. Paul law left police and other officials in charge of determining which symbols and which acts offended people in ways that crossed the line between "legal" and "illegal."

"BEDROCK PRINCIPLE"

At the hearing Cleary argued that the St. Paul ordinance targeted nonverbal symbolic expression, which is

---

protected under the First Amendment. He cited one case, *Collin v. Smith*, in which the Seventh Circuit Court of Appeals ruled that the village of Skokie, Illinois, where many Holocaust survivors and relatives of Holocaust victims lived, could not prohibit a group of neo-Nazis from displaying the Nazi symbol in a demonstration in front of the village hall. The court ruled that the local ordinance barring materials that promoted hatred on the basis of heritage was unconstitutional.

Cleary also discussed two U.S. Supreme Court decisions on flag burning, one delivered only weeks before, which struck down a federal law that had made burning the American flag a crime. In the first case, *Texas v. Johnson* (1989), the high court established that the First Amendment protects protesters who burn the flag as a political protest. The Court delivered a similar ruling on June 21, 1990, in *United States v. Eichman*.

In *Texas v. Johnson* the Supreme Court, in a decision written by Justice William J. Brennan Jr., tossed out a Texas law that barred burning the U.S. flag. The case involved a protester named Gregory Johnson, who burned an American flag in 1984 as part of a protest during the Republican National Convention in Dallas. The controversial split decision affirmed that the First Amendment protects actions expressing political views even if onlookers are offended.

"If there is a bedrock principle underlying the First

Gregory Johnson holds a flag sent to him by an unknown well-wisher in New York on June 28, 1989, to celebrate his victory in a Supreme Court case that established the right of protesters to burn the U.S. flag as an expression of their views.

Amendment, it is that the Government may not prohibit the expression of an idea simply because society finds the idea itself offensive or disagreeable," Justice Brennan wrote in the 5-to-4 ruling. The dissenter's right to express himself is a fundamental right guaranteed to all citizens. As such it outweighs the state's interest in banning desecration of the nation's symbol. Furthermore, the justice declared, the Constitution bars the state from penalizing Johnson on the basis of "the content of the message he conveyed."

In stating his case for Viktora, Cleary quoted Justice Anthony M. Kennedy's concurrence in the *Johnson* case on the difficulty of delivering controversial decisions when even those who support the defendant's arguments find the offense repugnant. "The hard fact is that sometimes we must make decisions we do not like," Justice Kennedy wrote. "We make them because they are right, right in the sense that the law and the Constitution, as we see them, compel the result."

A DECISION AND AN APPEAL

Swayed by the Supreme Court's flag-burning decisions, Judge Charles A. Flinn Jr. ruled on July 16 that St. Paul's ordinance, which could be used to prohibit legitimate political protest, was too broad. Although sharing Justice Kennedy's "great agony" in ruling for a defendant accused of such a repugnant act, the judge said he could not allow the city to infringe on the First Amendment right of free speech. Following the Supreme Court's edict about laws that were too broad, Judge Flinn rejected the city's ordinance and dismissed the disorderly conduct charge against Viktora. He said the flag-burning cases "follow almost to a tee the issue . . . raised by [Viktora]" and provided a "bright line" that led him to find that the ordinance was unconstitutional.

Laura Jones and others took issue with the ruling, arguing that burning a cross differed greatly from setting a flag on fire. "Cross burning is a direct threat, flag burning is just a protest," Mrs. Jones told reporters. "When you go on somebody's property and threaten them, that's not protected speech." St. Paul mayor Jim Scheibel expressed similar views: "Burning a cross more than frightens people. It drives people out of their home and makes them frightened for their safety and security."

In response, the county attorney's office decided to appeal the ruling and asked the Minnesota Supreme Court to expedite the process by allowing the case to be heard without going through the court of appeals. In August the state high court announced that it would review the case ahead of others on the docket. Viktora's public defender, Cleary, with the help of attorney Michael Cromett, decided to continue representing the teenager during the appeal, even though the county had no money to pay for the attorneys' services. The decision would cut into their own law practices and threaten their finances, but they forged ahead.

On December 4, 1990, Cleary and Steven DeCoster, a lawyer with the Ramsey County Attorney's office, argued the case before the state's highest court. DeCoster, representing St. Paul, began with a description of the cross burning and a discourse on the need for hate-crime laws. If the court found the St. Paul ordinance to be too broad, DeCoster said, the judges should interpret the law to apply only to "fighting words" rather than throw it out altogether. The U.S. Supreme Court had ruled that "fighting words"—those that "inflict injury or tend to incite an immediate breach of the peace"—did not merit protection under the First Amendment and could be prohibited or punished.

Cleary focused on the law itself, not his client's actions. He argued that the ordinance allowed officials to punish unpopular and controversial speech and expression—an encroachment on the First Amendment's guarantee of free speech. Even well-intentioned laws aimed at hate crimes and despicable symbols of intolerance such as cross burning should not be permitted to weaken the First Amendment, he said. He noted that the court would not condone cross burning by rejecting the law. Instead, the justices would send "a clear message" that lawmakers could not pass laws that suppressed "politically unpopular expression" while claiming to keep the peace.

COURT REINTERPRETATION OF ST. PAUL LAW

Six weeks later, on January 18, 1991, the Minnesota Supreme Court unanimously rejected the lower court's ruling and upheld the city ordinance. "Burning a cross in the yard of an African American family's home is deplorable conduct that the city of St. Paul may without question prohibit," the decision began. "The burning of a cross is itself an unmistakable symbol of violence and hatred based on virulent notions of racial supremacy."

The decision, written by Justice Esther M. Tomljanovich, noted that Viktora had challenged the ordinance on the ground that it was too broad, potentially censoring "so many constitutionally protected activities . . . that it must be completely invalidated." The court disagreed. While acknowledging that courts had to strike down overbroad laws when they

Justice Esther Tomljanovich

created "an unnecessary risk of chilling free speech," the Minnesota justices determined that such "strong medicine" was not necessary in the case of St. Paul's statute. They chose instead to narrow the law's focus, so that it would apply only to "fighting words" not covered under the First Amendment. The newly interpreted law, the decision noted, would not jeopardize the rights of those whose speech was legitimately protected by the Constitution. It would apply to cross burnings such as the one at the heart of the *R.A.V.* case.

Justice Tomljanovich cited the Supreme Court's decision in *Texas v. Johnson*, the flag-burning case in which the Court rejected a state law banning such activity. Even though the Court threw out the Texas law, Tomljanovich pointed out, it allowed states to prohibit

"FIGHTING WORDS" AND FREE SPEECH

Since its first decisions on free speech and the First Amendment, the Supreme Court has recognized that Americans do not have an absolute right to express themselves. In various rulings through the years, the Court has concluded that the First Amendment does not protect certain categories of speech or expressive acts. Among these exceptions to free speech are defamation and libel (false and damaging statements spoken or written), obscenity, causing panic or a disturbance of the peace, incitement to crime, "fighting words," and sedition (inciting a revolt against the government).

The 1942 case of *Chaplinsky v. New Hampshire* revolved around a man who called a city marshal a "damned racketeer" and "a damned fascist" in public. He was convicted of violating a New Hampshire law that made it a crime to address "any offensive, derisive or annoying word to any other person who is lawfully in any street or other public place," or "call him by any offensive or derisive name." The Court ruled that "fighting words"—"those which by their very utterance inflict injury or tend to incite an immediate breach of the peace"—had no First Amendment protections. Such words, Justice Frank Murphy wrote for the unanimous Court, had little or no value and did not further the "exposition of ideas." Therefore such words could be banned under the Constitution in the interest of "order and morality." Although the Court has never overruled the decision, it has repeatedly tightened the circumstances under which the "fighting words" doctrine applies. And it has not upheld any conviction on that basis since *Chaplinsky*.

The Court revised the standard of "fighting words" in 1949 in *Terminiello v. Chicago*. The case involved a fiery speech, in which Arthur W. Terminiello, a former priest, had attacked Jews and several U.S. officials, inflaming a Chicago crowd and creating a disturbance. In upholding Terminiello's right to address the crowd, the Court ruled that speech could be restricted only when it was "likely to produce a clear and present danger of a serious substantive evil that rises far above public inconvenience, annoyance, or unrest." Justice William O. Douglas, in his majority opinion, went so far as to suggest that such disturbances benefited the nation: "[Free speech] may indeed best serve its high purpose when it induces a condition of unrest, creates dissatisfaction with conditions as they are, or even stirs people to anger."

Again, in 1969 in the case of *Brandenburg v. Ohio*, the Court set a new standard for restricting speech, this time allowing government to punish speech only in emergencies when the words would result in "imminent lawless action."

The Court in 2003, in *Virginia v. Black*, clarified that true threats were among forms of expression not covered by the First Amendment. In the majority decision written by Justice Sandra Day O'Connor, the Court struck down a Virginia law banning all cross burnings but ruled that such acts could be prosecuted if proven to be an attempt to intimidate. True threats, the justice said, were "those statements where the speaker means to communicate a serious expression of an intent to commit an act of unlawful violence to a particular individual or group of individuals."

"fighting words" or expressive conduct "likely to provoke imminent lawless action." Therefore, the Minnesota court reasoned, if the St. Paul ordinance applied only to "fighting words" and actions that incited "imminent lawless action," it would fall within the Constitution.

The judges acknowledged that the St. Paul law "should have been more carefully drafted." They asserted, however, under the new interpretation, the ordinance would affect "only those expressions of hatred and resorts to bias-motivated personal abuse" not protected under the First Amendment. The ruling closed the loopholes under which officials could have charged political dissenters under the law or others whose speech was protected. In the future, the law would reach only those whose bias-motivated conduct threatened public safety and order.

The ruling left the charges against Viktora intact.

CHAPTER THREE

APPEAL TO THE SUPREME COURT

THE RULING BY THE MINNESOTA SUPREME Court left Robert Viktora and his attorneys with two choices: accept the verdict and go to trial or appeal to the U.S. Supreme Court.

Filing an appeal with the Supreme Court is far from a guarantee that a case will be heard. Each year the Supreme Court receives thousands of such requests, called petitions for *certiorari*, and most are rejected outright. Some are ruled improper. Others don't qualify to be heard by the Supreme Court for other reasons. The remaining petitions are reviewed by the Court's clerks, who rate them and pass along the most likely cases to the justices. To be considered by the Court, a case must receive the votes of at least four justices. The Court hears up to one hundred cases from October to late June or early July. An attorney's chances of having his or her case selected are slim.

To win a spot on the Court's docket, a case must fall within one of the following categories:

- Disputes between states and the federal government or between two or more states. The Court also reviews cases involving ambassadors, consuls, and foreign ministers.
- Appeals from state courts that have ruled on a federal question.
- Appeals from federal appeals courts (about two-thirds of all requests fall into this category).

Those few lawyers lucky enough to win a hearing before the Court then spend the next months preparing exhaustive briefs—documents that describe the incidents leading to the court proceeding, outline the issues involved, discuss the lower court hearings, present arguments, and cite past Supreme Court decisions that support the client's interests.

After the justices have reviewed the briefs, the lawyers for each side present their oral arguments. Legal experts have often said that a lawyer cannot win a case during oral argument, but he or she can lose a case there. A poor performance before the justices certainly never helps an attorney's case. Neither Edward Cleary nor his colleague, Michael Cromett, had ever appeared before the U.S. Supreme Court. In fact, Cleary's first appearance before the Minnesota Supreme Court had been to argue the *R.A.V.* case. When he conferred with more experienced lawyers, they suggested he turn the case over to them or allow others to argue before the Court.

SEEKING A HEARING

Cleary's father, a respected attorney himself, died two and a half weeks after the state court delivered its decision in the *R.A.V.* case. Absorbed in family affairs and trying to get his private law practice back on track, Cleary had serious doubts about committing himself to the overwhelming workload a Supreme Court challenge would entail. Michael Cromett, too, was feeling the pressure. Since the county had no funds to carry on an appeal, the two lawyers would have to work without pay. In the end, despite these difficulties and the advice of other attorneys, the two men decided to continue with the case. Cleary and Cromett made this choice because they believed in the sanctity of free speech and they did not want the Minnesota decision, which they considered to be flawed, to serve as the authority in future cases. "The First Amendment would not cease to exist," Cleary later wrote in his book about the case, *Beyond the Burning Cross*, "but we believed its key guarantee of freedom of speech would erode over time."

In their petition for *certiorari*, Cleary and Cromett focused on two points. First, they argued that the St. Paul ordinance violated the Constitution because it was too broad and too vague. As a result, the ordinance restricted too much speech that was protected under the First Amendment. Second, they contended that the Minnesota court's ruling did not "fix" the law. The ordinance as interpreted by the state court still depended on the content of a person's speech or expression. The First Amendment, the lawyers wrote in their petition, did not allow the government to pick and choose which sentiments expressed by Americans should be censured. The city ordinance, the lawyers wrote, violated the First Amendment because "its literal wording punishes and may deter a significant range of protected expression." A democracy had to tolerate "varied political viewpoints," even if they disgusted the majority of Americans. Under the Constitution, symbols such as the Nazi swastika or a burning cross could not be banned merely because most people found them offensive.

Cleary noted a growing trend in the country toward suppressing unpopular points of view. "Clearly there has been a nationwide movement towards stifling expressive conduct that the majority finds offensive or demeaning." He urged the Court to determine "the boundaries between expressive conduct protected under the First Amendment and permissible restrictions on such expressions."

On April 11, 1991, the lawyers filed their request for a hearing. The following month the Minnesota Civil Liberties Union (MCLU), the state chapter of the American Civil Liberties Union, filed a separate brief in support of Cleary's position. Advocates on both sides of an issue may file their own briefs arguing for or against the matter at hand. A party who files one of these briefs is said to be an *amicus curiae*, a Latin phrase meaning "friend of the court." Both parties in the suit or the Court must approve the submission of these so-called *amicus* briefs. Government agencies—such as the U.S. Department of Justice or the individual states—do not need such permission. In this case, the county attorney's office rejected the MCLU's request to file a petition for the appellant, but the Court granted permission. Often *amicus curiae* briefs contain analyses, information, or personal stories that add to the Court's understanding of the issue under discussion.

Tom Foley, the prosecutor, defended the city's ordinance. The forty-two-year-old Foley had served as a state assistant attorney general and deputy commissioner of corrections before winning election as Ramsey County attorney in 1978. In that role, he led the St. Paul legal team in the *R.A.V.* case. In Minnesota, all legal matters involving juveniles come under the jurisdiction of the county attorney.

On May 7 Foley's office filed a brief opposing

Cleary's petition and asking the Court not to hear the case. "Burning a cross is an unmistakable symbol of violence and hatred," he told reporters after filing the brief. "Society has a right to intervene and censor that type of activity." Steven Freeman, a lawyer advocating for hate-crime laws for the Anti-Defamation League

Ramsey County attorney Tom Foley

of B'nai B'rith, said the activities targeted by the law should be considered "terrorism" rather than expression or speech. "I would hope the Supreme Court would look at this case and say that burning a cross in the middle of the night in a black family's yard is far different [from] burning a flag in front of a public building to express a political opinion."

CASE ON THE DOCKET

On June 10, 1991, the U.S. Supreme Court announced it would consider Viktora's appeal. The high court's decision to take on the case meant that the justices would explore once again the reaches of the First Amendment and decide whether its protections extended to hate speech. In the past few years, the Court had issued a number of controversial decisions on free speech, including the rulings on flag burning, that divided the justices as well as the country.

Advocates of hate-speech laws feared that the decision in the two flag-burning cases might reflect the Court's leaning in favor of First Amendment claims. The St. Paul legal team, however, had hopes that the outcome would be different in the city's hate-speech case. For one thing, Justice Brennan, the Court's leading advocate for First Amendment rights, had been replaced by David H. Souter. Appointed in 1990 by Republican president George H. W. Bush, Souter had no track record on First Amendment issues and had been dubbed by the press the "stealth justice." Further, the advocates pushing for hate-crime statutes contended that cross burning and other hateful activities focused on threats and fear, not politics. "The crime involved here is easily distinguishable from flag burning," said Steven Freeman of the Anti-Defamation League of B'nai B'rith. "The motive for cross burning is to intimidate, not to convey a political message."

Free-speech proponents, however, believed the St. Paul ordinance demonstrated the dangers inherent in speech control. They hoped that a Supreme Court decision in the *R.A.V.* case would help curb the campaigns that had sprung up on college campuses across the nation to ban speech that officials deemed not "politically correct" or that targeted certain minorities. Many of these

HATE SPEECH ON CAMPUS

In 1990, when the cross burning in the *R.A.V.* case occurred, there were seventy-five codes or policies to regulate hate speech at U.S. colleges. By the time the U.S. Supreme Court heard arguments in *R.A.V. v. St. Paul* a year later, the number of colleges with hate-speech codes in place had grown to more than three hundred. A corollary study revealed that college students filed four times as many reports of harassment in 1990 as they had in 1985.

Some codes ban speech or conduct that intimidates people, offends them, or creates a hostile environment. Other codes target behavior that intentionally creates emotional distress. Some colleges issue a general prohibition against all harassment and threats. Educators maintain that the codes protect minority students and create a more civil atmosphere on campus. By banning hate speech, universities say they are teaching students to rely on facts and rational arguments when expressing their views, rather than hateful language that provokes violence. The codes also reinforce universities' commitment to civil rights and ensure that minority students can pursue their education without being intimidated. Hate speech, code advocates say, inspires fear in targeted students and interferes with their ability to study and attend classes.

"Hate speech," writes Ryan Heman in the *Tufts Daily*, the Boston university's independent student newspaper, "degrades a person's humanity, worth and sense of self. It is not something easy to get over. . . . It creates a hostile environment that perpetuates discrimination against traditionally marginalized groups, and free speech policies merely institutionalize the ability of people to hurt others."

Critics of the codes see them as unacceptable restrictions on free speech that serve only to censor opinions and silence expression. They say banning speech does not solve the problem of bias, which needs to be dealt with directly, in workshops, forums, classes, and everyday encounters. When colleges allow students to express their views, even hateful ones, bigotry is exposed and people can take a stand against such attitudes. "Universities ought to stop restricting speech and start teaching," says Ira Glasser, executive director of the American Civil Liberties Union. The ACLU maintains that colleges can deal with harassment, violence, and bullying by punishing hateful conduct rather than trying to gag students.

Federal and state courts have struck down speech codes at several colleges, including Central Michigan University and Stanford University. The rulings applied only to public institutions, but many private colleges also revisited their policies in the wake of the court rulings and widespread criticism of the codes by free-speech advocates. A number of colleges looked at approaches to the problem of hate crimes that did not target speech or expression. After a student committed suicide in 2010 following harassment by his roommate, Rutgers University, in New Jersey, introduced Project Civility, a two-year program designed to "encourage small acts of courtesy, compassion, and respect" and to reduce hostility between those of different cultures, races, and viewpoints. Other colleges and universities have set up similar programs. At Arizona State University, the Campus Environment Team, made up of faculty and staff members, resolves disputes and promotes diversity and "a positive, harmonious campus environment."

In some cases, however, colleges take their efforts to maintain civility to extreme lengths. One such incident occurred in 1993 when a white male student at the University of Pennsylvania yelled, "Shut up, you water buffalo," to a group of noisy, mostly black female students who were creating a disturbance late at night outside his dorm. As a result of complaints by the women, the student was charged with racial harassment under the school's speech code. The incident attracted a flood of ridicule and resulted in the university's revising its speech policies. "I think the case exposed Penn's hypocrisy, its repression, its double standards and the nightmare of a speech code at a major university," said Alan Kors, a history professor and free-speech advocate who advised the student during legal proceedings.

Alexander Tsesis, associate professor of law at Loyola University Chicago School of Law, believes colleges can establish policies that meet constitutional demands while preventing threats and acts that intimidate students. "Hate speech," he asserts, "is unrelated to the pursuit of truth, and the interest in public order justifies reasonable limitations on its dissemination on campuses."

advocates believed the hate-speech codes infringed on free speech. Laurence Tribe, professor of constitutional law at Harvard Law School and a renowned liberal scholar on the Constitution, said the case was an important one because it came at a time when officials were curbing speech that did harm. "The First Amendment is almost always tested with speech that is profoundly divisive or painful," Tribe said. "But if you start making exceptions, and suppressing speech that is hurtful, those exceptions will swallow free speech, and the only speech that will be left protected will be abstracted, emotionally lightweight speech that doesn't pack any wallop."

STATING THEIR CASE

On July 23, 1991, Cleary filed his brief with the Supreme Court. In it he focused on the wording of the ordinance and his contention that it violated the Constitution because it was too broad. Even with the Minnesota Supreme Court's interpretation of the law, Cleary held that the ordinance was still too vague and still relied on an examination of the content of speech (or expression) to determine whether it was motivated by certain biases (race, religion, gender). The St. Paul ordinance allowed government to punish people based on officials' interpretation of the offenders' motivations. The Constitution did not allow the state to specify which opinions were "disfavored" and which were not, he argued.

Cleary included a passage from Robert Bolt's play, *A Man for All Seasons*, the story of Sir Thomas More's decision to defy King Henry VIII and face execution rather than abandon his principles. In the play, More responds to a statement by his son-in-law that he would "cut down every law in England" to capture the Devil:

> Thomas More: Oh? And when the last law was down, and the Devil turned round on you— where would you hide, the laws all being flat? . . . If you cut them down . . . d'you really think you could stand upright in the winds that would blow then? Yes, I'd give the Devil benefit of law, for my own safety's sake.

The passage, Cleary believed, illustrated exactly his point that free-speech protections must cover all or they will not be around to cover anyone. The lawyer concluded his brief by noting that the St. Paul ordinance might restrict some "offensive" expression by cross burners and the like, but it had the potential to "chill" the protected speech of many others. "The result may well be the silencing of political debate, the encouraging of orthodoxy, and the endangering of the individual's right to dissent," he wrote.

St. Paul's brief, filed by the county attorney's office, focused on three arguments. First, the writers, Tom Foley

Sir Thomas More

and Steven DeCoster, maintained that the state supreme court's interpretation of the law brought it into compliance with the Constitution. By limiting the banned conduct to "fighting words," the newly interpreted ordinance applied only to speech or conduct not protected by the First Amendment.

Second, the lawyers contended that the city had a "compelling interest" in protecting minorities from the effects of hate crimes and protecting their human rights. Members of these groups, they noted, had been victimized for years by words and deeds aimed at degrading and vilifying them. The ordinance, they argued, helped "to ensure the basic human rights of members of groups that have historically been subjected to discrimination."

The third argument presented in the brief was that even if the city ordinance required officials to examine offenders' motivations (and thus was content based), a law targeted specifically at hate crimes was needed to let minority groups know that the majority of its citizens did not condone such conduct.

A surprising mix of interest groups backed Cleary's position, while an equally unusual mix of states and organizations lined up against it. The issue pitted free-speech proponents against civil rights advocates and joined the American Jewish Congress (AJC) in the same cause supported by the Patriots Defense Foundation (PDF), which represented white supremacists. Seven organizations filed four briefs supporting Cleary's First Amendment claims. In addition to the AJC and the PDF, Cleary's position was supported by the Association of American Publishers, Freedom to Read (the American Library Association's legal arm, founded to defend First Amendment rights), the Center for Individual Rights (a conservative group dedicated to defending individual liberties), the Minnesota Civil Liberties Union, and the American Civil Liberties Union.

On the other side, attorneys general representing seventeen states submitted *amicus* briefs asking the Court to uphold St. Paul's hate-crime law. Groups as diverse as the Anti-Defamation League of B'nai B'rith, the National Association for the Advancement of Col-

Protesters march against hate speech on the University of Oregon campus in Eugene, Oregon, in 2010. The university provided a meeting place for the Pacifica Forum, which served as a venue for speakers who deny that the Holocaust took place. The Southern Poverty Law Center has labeled the forum a hate group.

ored People (NAACP), the liberal People for the American Way, and the conservative Criminal Justice Legal Foundation (advocating swift punishment for criminals) also supported the St. Paul ordinance. Additional briefs on the side of the ordinance included those filed by Asian and gay and lesbian groups, the National Lawyers Guild, the YWCA, the United Automobile Workers union, and the liberal Center for Constitutional Rights, cofounded by the radical lawyer William Kunstler. Kunstler, who had defended Gregory Johnson in the 1989 flag-burning case, disagreed with the center's position in the *R.A.V.* case. Fifty-one groups in all filed ten briefs advocating for the hate-crime law.

Oral arguments in the case were set for December 4, 1991. By that time, Viktora had reached his nineteenth birthday, but because he was a minor when the matter first came to court, the original name of the case, *R.A.V. v. St. Paul*, continued to be used.

A NEW JUSTICE

Seventeen days after the Court agreed to hear *R.A.V.*, Justice Thurgood Marshall announced his retirement from the bench. Marshall, who had argued the school segregation cases as a lawyer for the NAACP before the Supreme Court in the 1960s, was a strong proponent of civil liberties, including free speech. In the majority opinion in an obscenity case, he wrote, "Our whole constitutional heritage rebels at the thought of giving government the power to control men's minds." As the Court's first and (at the time) only African American member and a former NAACP leader, Justice Marshall would have been sympathetic to the Jones family, but because he did not weigh in on the matter, his vote, had he remained on the Court, must be a matter of speculation.

After a lengthy confirmation process, the Senate approved President George H. W. Bush's appointment of Clarence Thomas, a conservative African American judge, to fill the seat left vacant by Marshall's resignation. The new justice assumed office on October 23, 1991, scarcely six weeks before the lawyers would argue *R.A.V. v. St. Paul* before the Court. When it came to the First Amendment, Thomas, like Souter, was an enigma. No one could predict which way he would vote on the upcoming case.

Russell and Laura Jones stand outside the Supreme Court building in Washington, D.C., after hearing oral arguments on their cross-burning case.

CHAPTER FOUR

BEFORE THE COURT

A COLD DRIZZLE HAD LEFT THE NATION'S capital sodden, but the sun greeted the lawyers in the *R.A.V. v. St. Paul* case as they climbed the steps to the U.S. Supreme Court in Washington, D.C. This day, December 4, 1991, would mark the culmination of their efforts to win the Court's favor.

The crier shouted "Oyez, oyez, oyez," the Old English version of "Hear ye," to mark the opening of the Court session. The room became still as Chief Justice William Rehnquist, followed by the eight associate justices, filed through the heavy red velvet curtains separating their chambers from the court-room. Selected members of the public and the press, along with guests and legal staff, filled the mahogany seats in front of the bench. Edward Cleary had saved a seat for his client, Robert Viktora, the teen accused in the case. Like many others at the heart of a Supreme

Court appeal, the young man chose not to attend the oral arguments, but Russell and Laura Jones, the couple whose lawn had been the site of the burning cross, sat quietly waiting for the arguments to begin. Behind the room's majestic columns, crowded into chairs at the back of the room, visitors watched and listened to the proceedings in shifts, with each new group replaced after five minutes to make way for others in line.

Exactly one year before, Cleary had argued the case before the Minnesota Supreme Court. He hoped the results would be different this time. Ramsey County attorney Thomas J. Foley, the government prosecutor representing St. Paul, hoped the high court would follow the state court's lead in ruling that the city ordinance was a legitimate way to control hate crimes.

FIRST AMENDMENT ARGUMENTS

Since the appeal had been filed on behalf of Viktora, Cleary rose first to present his case. The lawyer opened his oral argument with the statement, "Each generation must reaffirm the guarantee of the First Amendment with the hard cases." The case of his client, he told the justices, represented a "hard case" in which the conduct was "reprehensible" and "abhorrent." He noted, however, that he was not in court to defend such conduct but to test "whether or not there is room for the freedom for the thought that we hate."

In response to questions from Justice Sandra Day O'Connor, Cleary acknowledged that the Minnesota Supreme Court tried to redefine the St. Paul law so that it met First Amendment requirements. Even with the court's new interpretation, though, the statute opened "a hole to the First Amendment," Cleary contended.

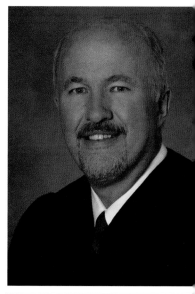

Attorney Edward Cleary

The Minnesota court ruling, he said, allowed much more latitude in banning free expression than the Supreme Court had permitted in either the *Chaplinsky* or the *Brandenburg* case. The *Chaplinsky* ruling, which bars "fighting words," limits expression or speech only when it provokes or promises to provoke "an immediate breach of peace," Cleary noted. Likewise, the standard set for free-speech barriers in *Brandenburg v. Ohio* allows government to punish speech only in situations where the words will result in "imminent lawless action." (For example, a person could be arrested if he grabbed a torch and urged a mob to set fire to a house right then. But his speech would be protected if he merely said to an acquaintance that so-and-so deserved to have his house burned down.)

The St. Paul ordinance, on the other hand, censured speech or expression that a person knows "arouses anger, alarm or resentment in others on the basis of race, color, creed, religion or gender." Cleary argued that the St. Paul standard came close to allowing a ban on words that one person might consider outrageous. The Supreme Court had already outlawed that standard in ruling against evangelist Jerry Falwell in his suit against a men's magazine, decided in 1988. In *Hustler Magazine Inc. v. Falwell*, the Court said that Falwell could not collect damages merely because he was offended by an outrageous parody that appeared in the magazine.

Justice Antonin Scalia observed that the St. Paul law did not punish speech or expression that caused "alarm or resentment" for reasons other than those based on "race, color, creed, religion, or gender."

Cleary assured the Court that he did not intend to make light of the victims' fear when they witnessed the burning crosses. The state could have punished the teens under "significant and hard and tough laws." Instead, officials chose to pursue the cross burners under a law that addressed expression rather than conduct. That law targeted the content, or meaning, of certain speech or activity, which allowed officials to pick and choose which messages were worthy of censure. For example, Cleary said, the Minnesota law could prevent the display of the Jewish Star of David because it might be considered an example of "fighting words" to some people. "It's a paternalistic idea, and the problem that we have is that the Government must not betray neutrality," Cleary said.

Robert Viktora's attorney argued that under the St. Paul ordinance, the display of the Star of David, seen here on the Israeli national flag, might be considered provocative and could be prohibited.

The lawyer made it clear that he was not condoning or defending hateful actions: "The debate in this case is not about the wisdom of eradicating intolerance, the debate is about the method of reaching that goal." A different law, which did not depend on the viewpoint expressed by the action, might well be constitutional and could be used to punish cross burning, he acknowledged. The well-meaning community members who try to control hate speech through such laws endanger the protections guaranteed by the First Amendment, Cleary asserted. "I believe that this is the hour of danger for the First Amendment," he said.

In responding to questioning by Justice Scalia, Cleary took issue with the Minnesota Supreme Court's assertion that swastikas and burning crosses were always symbols of hatred—a judgment that could be interpreted as calling for a ban on those symbols. Banning symbols or certain words, however, would amount to censoring expression protected under the First Amendment, Cleary contended.

Justice Scalia pushed further. "[B]ut why is it that there can't be such a thing as a fighting word per se, a kind of a word that would be likely to provoke a violent reaction from an ordinary person?" Scalia asked. Otherwise, he noted, such words could be censured only if those who heard them were likely to react violently. For example, a crowd of pacifists who heard the same words would not respond to them with physical aggression.

Cleary responded that prohibiting certain symbols or "fighting" words "could lead to a ban on symbolic behavior in such a fashion that a great deal of expression would be prohibited." If government could automatically ban swastikas and burning crosses, it could ban any symbol that someone believed was a symbol of hate.

Chief Justice Rehnquist noted that the Court's decision in *Texas v. Johnson* in 1989 allowing flag burning as a means of protest bolstered the argument against a ban on hate symbols or inflammatory words.

Justice Anthony Kennedy asked if the law applied when listeners feared harm but not imminent danger from a cross burning or other act of expression. Cleary replied that other laws—that did not judge conduct based on viewpoint—could deal with such threats. With that, he stepped back to his seat, reserving the last few minutes of his argument until his opponent had presented St. Paul's case.

ST. PAUL'S CASE

Foley rose to face the Court. Taking a position opposite that of Cleary, he would argue that the St. Paul law did indeed meet the requirements of *Chaplinsky v. New Hampshire* and *Brandenburg v. Ohio*.

Before Foley could begin his arguments, Justice Harry Blackmun, who had spent his childhood and much of his early legal career in St. Paul, quizzed the lawyer on the location of the cross burning to the amusement of the audience. After the laughter subsided, Foley addressed Chief Justice Rehnquist. "The First Amendment was never intended to protect an individual who burns a cross in the middle of the night in the fenced yard of an African American family's home," he stated. The city, he added, had every right to ban such activity and prosecute those responsible for it.

The state's high court had interpreted the city's law in a way that met constitutional concerns, Foley said. Under the ruling, the law applied only to conduct that inflicted injury, tended to incite "an immediate breach of the peace," or provoked "imminent lawless action." Foley noted that the U.S. Supreme Court had allowed officials to punish such conduct—or speech or expression—under its rulings in *Chaplinsky* and *Brandenburg*. Unless the Court was willing to overturn those two decisions, Foley said, it must uphold the St. Paul law.

Justice O'Connor noted that the municipal ordinance could not be content neutral because the harm the law addressed was based on specific criteria: race, color, creed, religion, or gender. To determine whether the expression harmed anyone based on those categories, officials had to examine what the speech was about. Foley disagreed with the justice's assertion. But he said that even if the law required officials to examine the content of words or expressions, the state had a "compelling" purpose to do so in order to protect its citizens and preserve order and public safety. Because the ordinance dealt with "fighting words," Foley said the conduct or expression would not be protected under the First Amendment anyway.

Justice Scalia asked why the law targeted only race, color, creed, religion, or gender. "If you want to prohibit fighting words, prohibit fighting words. But why [limit it only to] fighting words for these particular purposes?"

Foley replied that "bias-motivated conduct and violence" was much more harmful to citizens, but Scalia cut him off. "That's a political judgment," the justice said. Other people, he said, might have equally strong feelings about philosophy or another topic; the city could have accomplished the same thing by dropping the hate-crime language. "Just say [conduct] that arouses anger, alarm, or resentment in others, period," the justice suggested.

Foley saw no need to make further modifications to the law. He insisted the law as interpreted by the Minnesota Supreme Court met constitutional requirements.

In response to questions by Justices Souter and Blackmun, Foley asserted that the circumstances surrounding an act would determine whether it violated the St. Paul ordinance. For example, the law would not apply to a cross burning in a public forum or as part of a political parade. The action, he said, had to do more than offend onlookers; it had to "inflict injury or cause an immediate breach of the peace" to run afoul of the law—and to meet the Court's requirements stipulated in the *Chaplinsky* decision. For the Joneses, Foley said, burning a cross in their yard was "more than just outrageous conduct." It caused "direct harm" to them and produced "fear, intimidation, threats, and coercion." In addition, he said, the cross burning threatened the peace.

The lawyer asserted that activities motivated by bias and hatred have a much more harmful effect than similar conduct with no such motives. Burning a cross at the home of an African American family, he said, goes far beyond simple trespassing or minor arson.

Foley's comments raised a question in Justice Scalia's mind. He asked why the law would not also cover the situation of vandals lighting a cross in front of a home for people with mental illness, with a sign saying "Mentally ill out." Foley acknowledged that unless officials added another category to the law to cover disability, it would not apply in Scalia's hypothetical case. That did not sit well with the justice. "If you are concerned about breaches of the public peace, if it's a fighting words problem, why is it okay for the State to have the public peace broken for that reason?" he asked Foley.

The prosecutor replied that cities and states do not address all wrongs at the same time. He also noted that cross burning had particular historical significance to African Americans as "a precursor to violence and hatred in this country." He agreed with Justice O'Connor's suggestion that if the cross burning was not protected by the First Amendment, as he claimed, the city was free to pass laws punishing it in one instance and ignoring it in another. Defending the state supreme court's interpretation of the law, Foley reiterated the need to protect citizens from the "unmistakable threat" posed to African Americans by cross burning. "Terroristic conduct such as this can find no protection in the Constitution," he said.

Cleary used the remaining four minutes of his argument to stress the importance of the case and to point to the loophole it created in First Amendment protection of free speech: "This is a huge hole and I believe it really represses a great deal of expressive conduct." He noted that Minnesota's disorderly conduct law could have dealt with the situation in St. Paul. Instead, officials chose to punish the cross burners by charging them with violating the hate-crimes ordinance. That ordinance, in the words of Justice Scalia, "discriminate[d] on the basis of subject matter," allowing officials to punish those who expressed certain views. Cleary concluded by saying it would be "a sad irony" if the Court limited Americans' right of free expression at a time when countries in the former Soviet bloc were lifting repressive restrictions on their citizens' liberties.

Justice Sandra Day O'Connor

The U.S. Supreme Court in 1992 (*front row, from left*): Associate Justices John Paul Stevens and Byron White, Chief Justice William Rehnquist, Associate Justices Harry Blackmun and Sandra Day O'Connor; (*back row, from left*): Associate Justices David Souter, Antonin Scalia, Anthony Kennedy, and Clarence Thomas.

CHAPTER FIVE

THE DECISION

BY THE TIME *R.A.V. V. ST. PAUL* CAME BEFORE the U.S. Supreme Court, Utah, Wyoming, Nebraska, and Alaska were the only states that did not have some form of hate-crime or hate-speech law on the books. Hundreds of towns and cities had ordinances similar to the one questioned in *R.A.V.* Colleges and universities had adopted their own policies designed to curb hate speech and acts motivated by bias. Officials and school authorities across the nation awaited the Court's ruling in the *R.A.V.* case to see how it would affect their statutes and codes. It would take the Court almost seven months to reach a decision.

On June 22, 1992, the Supreme Court delivered a unanimous decision in favor of Robert A. Viktora. The ruling struck down the St. Paul ordinance and invalidated similar hate-crime and hate-speech statutes nationwide. The Court also validated the decision in *Texas v. Johnson* that allowed flag burning as a political statement and reaffirmed that the First Amendment protects symbolic expression, as well as the written word.

In making the announcement, Justice Antonin Scalia, who wrote the majority opinion, observed that the Court believed the petitioner's action in burning a cross in the Jones family's yard was "reprehensible." Nonetheless, the Court could not sacrifice the First Amendment to punish such an act. The decision did not say that the Constitution protects cross burning. St. Paul could have charged the offender under several valid laws, Scalia said, "without adding the First Amendment to the fire."

Although all nine justices voted to overturn the St. Paul law, the justices sharply divided on the validity of laws aimed at speech and crimes motivated by bias. Four of the justices supported three concurring opinions that at times sounded more like dissents.

Scalia's opinion, joined by associate justices Anthony M. Kennedy, David H. Souter, and Clarence Thomas, as well as Chief Justice William H. Rehnquist, rejected the St. Paul ordinance on the grounds that it targeted acts and expression based on their content. "The point of the First Amendment is that majority preferences must be expressed in some fashion other than silencing speech on the basis of its content," Scalia wrote. Although Scalia's opinion did not use the term "politically correct," it was easy to infer that the justice included speech codes aimed at suppressing offensive speech in his definition of "content-based discrimination."

The reason "fighting words" are excluded from the First Amendment's protection, Scalia said, was not that the words themselves communicate any particular idea, but because they "embodie[d] a particularly intolerable (and socially unnecessary) *mode* of expressing *whatever* idea the speaker wish[ed] to convey." He noted that the St. Paul law punished expression that contained a message motivated by a bias based on race, religion, or gender. The ordinance did not single out "'fighting words' that communicated ideas in a threatening . . . manner," Scalia said. Under the city's ordinance, behavior determined to be motivated by bias might also be punished for being "merely obnoxious." And behavior that was threatening but not motivated by racial, gender, or religious bias would escape the ordinance's penalties.

Scalia contended that the law was not too broad, as attorney Edward Cleary claimed, but that it was not broad enough. The law, Scalia said, punished only speech with a certain viewpoint. Therefore, he said, the St. Paul ordinance was unconstitutionally underinclusive and in fact content based. By censuring only expressions that conveyed "messages of racial, gender or religious intolerance," Scalia said, the law singled out certain words or symbols but not others that might be equally offensive. "Selectivity of this sort creates the possibility that the city

JUSTICE ANTONIN SCALIA

Lawyers arguing their cases before the U.S. Supreme Court expect to hear from Associate Justice Antonin Scalia. He asks more questions and makes more remarks than any of the other justices. And more often than not, his pointed barbs and wry comments bring laughter from the audience in the staid, red-draped courtroom.

Born in 1936 in New Jersey, Scalia was the only child of parents of Italian descent. His mother was

Associate Justice Antonin Scalia

a schoolteacher and his father, a language professor. At age five, Scalia moved with his family to Queens, New York. Known as "Nino" to his family, Scalia graduated at the top of his class from George-town University, then studied at Harvard Law School, where he also excelled. He and his wife, Maureen McCarthy, are the parents of nine children.

Scalia worked as an attorney, taught law, and served as counsel in the Richard Nixon and Ronald Reagan administrations. In 1982 he became a judge on the U.S. Court of Appeals, where he acquired a reputation as a strong conservative who believed in judicial restraint, the doctrine that courts have limited power and must rely on Congress and other governmental bodies to make policy. President Reagan nominated him to the Court in 1986 to fill the vacancy created when William Rehnquist became chief justice. At fifty, Scalia was the youngest member on the Court.

As an associate justice, Scalia has adopted what he calls "originalism," the theory that the Constitution is a fixed document whose meaning has not changed since ratification in 1788. He opposes other justices' attempts to interpret the Constitution in light of today's realities. While Scalia is among the most conservative justices on the Court, some of his votes have infuriated former supporters. He twice voted with the majority in striking down laws that banned flag desecration and, in the *R.A.V. v. St. Paul* case, he voted with other justices to overturn a hate-crime law, all in favor of free expression.

Scalia has at times been acerbic and pointed in his references to the writings of his colleagues. For example, in a 2004 concurrence on a ruling on abortion, which Scalia opposes, he said Justice Sandra Day O'Connor's majority decision could not "be taken seriously," that her reasoning was "particularly perverse," and that her ideas were "irrational." Justice Anthony Kennedy has felt the sting of Scalia's pen more than once. In a 1996 gay and lesbian civil rights case, Scalia wrote that Kennedy's majority opinion had "no foundation in American constitutional law, and barely pretends to." In a blistering attack on another Kennedy-authored opinion, Scalia accused the majority of delivering a "deliberately ambiguous set of suggestions" and "grasping authority that appellate courts are not supposed to have." He once derided a majority decision written by Justice John Paul Stevens as an "Alice in Wonderland determination" and dismissed Ruth Bader Ginsburg's words in a 1996 opinion as "fanciful," "misleading," and "irresponsible," forcing states to participate in "Supreme Court peek-a-boo." In 2007 he criticized the "meaningless and disingenuous distinctions" outlined in a majority opinion with which Scalia concurred. The rebuke was a clear dig at Chief Justice John G. Roberts Jr.

While his criticism of fellow justices can be harsh, they join in the merriment in response to some of Scalia's jokes in the courtroom and on the lecture circuit. One of his favorites is the bear story, which is paraphrased below:

Two hunters hear a growling sound outside their tent. When they open the tent flap, they see a huge grizzly bear and start running as fast as they can. One of the hunters, a bit overweight and lagging behind, says, "We'll never be able to outrun this bear." And the other guy, running up ahead, says, "I don't have to outrun the bear. I just have to outrun you."

He uses the anecdote to promote his theory of originalism over Justice Stephen Breyer's views. Scalia notes that he does not have to prove his views are the best. "I just have to show it's better than his [Breyer's view]," he tells listeners.

Pamela S. Karlan, a law professor at Stanford who has argued before the Supreme Court herself, says of the jovial Justice Scalia: "He plays to the crowd."

is seeking to handicap the expression of particular ideas," Scalia wrote. The First Amendment, he said, specifically bars Congress from silencing speech merely because the majority of the population does not like what it contains. Under the Constitution, Congress is prohibited from legislating or supporting certain viewpoints while punishing others. In 1925 the U.S. Supreme Court extended the ban on restricting speech to the state as well as the federal governments.

Scalia also noted the need to protect "symbols that communicate a message" as well as conduct that expresses a viewpoint, as burning the American flag had done in *Texas v. Johnson.*

Under Scalia's interpretation, practically all hate-crime laws, including the speech codes at public universities, would be struck down. Since almost all of them targeted conduct and expression motivated by certain biases (usually race, religion, gender, and sometimes sexual orientation) that could be determined only by examining the content of the expression or act, none would meet First Amendment requirements as set forth in Scalia's opinion.

Generally the First Amendment prohibits the government from censuring speech or expressive conduct based on its content. Just because the views expressed are objectionable and meet with the disapproval of officials or the majority of Americans is no reason to ban the words or punish the speaker. The Constitution does allow some restrictions on certain kinds of speech that fall outside the protection of the First Amendment, Scalia noted. People can be punished for uttering defamatory words, fighting words, libelous words, and obscene language. But, he asserted, officials still cannot favor one idea and punish another, even in cases of speech not protected under the First Amendment. For example, a city could prohibit words legally determined to be obscene. But it could not punish only those obscene words directed at local government officials. "The First Amendment does not permit St. Paul to impose special prohibitions on those speakers who express views on disfavored subjects," the justice noted.

Words slip and slide from one meaning to another, depending on the context and the situation in which they are uttered. Scalia noted that words or actions might not be protected in one case—burning a flag in an area where open fires are prohibited, for example—and allowed in another—burning a flag to express a particular political viewpoint. The Court established the line between an expressive action and a criminal act in the flag-burning case *Texas v. Johnson*. Even though Chief Justice Rehnquist had voted against the majority in that case, he signed on to Scalia's opinion in *R.A.V. v. St. Paul*.

The St. Paul ordinance, Scalia said, gives an advantage to those espousing tolerance of racial, religious, and gender diversity. For example, people with those views would not be punished for holding up a sign that was insulting to the mother of an opponent. But those on the other side, who expressed bias against those of another race, religion, or gender, would face arrest for holding up the same sign. "St. Paul has no such authority to license one side of a debate to fight freestyle, while requiring the other to follow Marquis of Queensbury Rules," Scalia wrote, alluding to the nineteenth-century code that mandated the use of gloves in boxing matches in Britain. In general, "Marquis of Queensbury Rules" means a fair code or standard of behavior.

The justice took issue with the claim that St. Paul's ordinance did not depend on the content of the speech but on the effects of the words or acts on the victims. He discounted the assertion by proponents of hate-crime laws that hate speech, because it evokes a painful history of abuse, inflicts injuries that are "qualitatively different" from the harm caused by nonbiased "fighting words." The theory, subscribed to by Justice John Paul Stevens in his concurrence, amounted to "wordplay," Scalia said. "What makes the anger, fear, sense of dishonor, etc. produced by violation of this ordinance distinct from the anger, fear, sense of dishonor, etc. produced by other fighting words is nothing other than the fact that it is caused by a distinctive idea, conveyed by a distinctive message. The First Amendment cannot be evaded that easily."

"RADICAL REVISION OF FIRST AMENDMENT LAW"

Four justices, in three concurrent opinions, agreed that the St. Paul law should be overturned, but they disagreed with Justice Scalia's argument that the ordinance should be rejected because it discriminated on the basis of content. Instead, they said the law was flawed because it prohibited too much material that was protected under the First Amendment. Conceivably, a hate-speech ordinance that did not restrict legitimate expression would meet constitutional requirements.

Justice Byron R. White, in an opinion supported by Justices Sandra Day O'Connor, Harry A. Blackmun, and (in part) Stevens, wrote that the St. Paul ordinance was "fatally overbroad" because, although it regulated some unprotected speech, it also criminalized "a substantial amount of expression that—however repugnant—is shielded by the First Amendment."

In his lengthy concurrence, White launched a sharp attack on the majority opinion, criticizing Scalia for basing the ruling on an "untried theory" that cast aside "long-established First Amendment doctrine." Scalia's reasoning in reaching the decision, White said, was "transparently wrong." Justice White argued that the Court's ban on expression in several cases involving speech not protected by the Constitution ("fighting words," libel, obscenity) implied that laws that considered content were allowable in certain circumstances.

The categories of unprotected speech are themselves based on content, White noted. Under Scalia's scheme, lawmakers could not regulate some fighting words more harshly than others. "Should the government want to criminalize certain fighting words, the Court now requires it to criminalize all fighting words," White said.

Scalia's "all-or-nothing-at-all approach" was "at odds with common sense," White argued. Such a system permitted, even invited, "the continuation of expressive conduct that, in this case, is evil and worthless in First Amendment terms," the justice wrote. The majority opinion, he said, "legitimates hate speech as a form of public discussion."

The approach used by Scalia left lawmakers concerned about hate speech with only two options, White said: pass a law that covered all fighting words, even though no problems had arisen involving such words except those motivated by bias, or pass no law at all. White discarded Scalia's view that without his system lawmakers could pass laws that discriminated against certain groups (banning libel only in cases involving city officials, for example). The Fourteenth Amendment's equal protection clause requires that laws treat Americans equally. Under the clause, White said, laws regulating unprotected speech have to be "rationally related to a legitimate government interest."

Traditionally the Supreme Court has allowed a state

to infringe on citizens' First Amendment rights if there is a compelling interest in doing so, if there is no better way to resolve the problem, and if the restrictions apply only to the problem at hand. For example, in the 1960s the Supreme Court ruled that a young man demonstrating against the Vietnam War could be punished for burning his draft card even though he argued that the action was his way of speaking out against the war and should be protected under the First Amendment. The high court declared that government had a compelling interest in maintaining an army during war, that draft cards were needed to further that end, and that the draft law infringed only minimally on the demonstrator's free speech because he could express his views in other ways.

White argued that St. Paul had a compelling interest in restricting expression motivated by "race, color, creed, religion or gender." The city's belief that hate speech inflicted more harm than other fighting words was "plainly reasonable," given the nation's "long and painful experience with discrimination," White said.

The problem with the ordinance lay not with its reliance on content (expression based on bias) but because it was too broad, White asserted. Even though the cross burning is not protected by the First Amendment, the St. Paul law interfered with other expression that is covered by free-speech guarantees—namely, words that merely offend or make others angry. "Although the ordinance reaches conduct that is unprotected," White concluded, "it also makes criminal expressive conduct that causes only hurt feelings, offense, or resentment, and is protected by the First Amendment."

White ended his opinion with a scathing assessment of the majority opinion, which he called "mischievous at best" and a "radical revision of First Amendment law."

OTHER VIEWS

Justice Blackmun wrote a brief opinion in which he opened the door to states and municipalities wanting to write hate-crime laws that would pass constitutional muster. Although he agreed with the majority opinion that the St. Paul ordinance should be invalidated because it restricted speech protected by the First Amendment, Blackmun said lawmakers should be able to enact valid laws to deal with hate speech. "I see no First Amendment values that are compromised by a law that prohibits hoodlums from driving minorities out of their homes by burning crosses on their lawn," he wrote, "but I see great harm in preventing the people of Saint Paul from specifically punishing the race-based fighting words that so prejudice their community."

He suggested that the majority had been "distracted from its proper mission" and in a "regrettable" move had weighed in on the issues of "politically correct speech"

and "cultural diversity." The case under review, Blackmun noted, did not touch on either topic.

Justice Stevens, in another lengthy concurrence, part
of which was joined by Justices White and Blackmun,
also made the case for laws that punished hate crimes
more severely than other crimes. "Conduct that creates
special risks or causes special harms may be prohibited
by special rules," he stated. For example, a person who
ignites a fire near a gasoline storage tank—an extremely
dangerous act—would face harsher penalties than someone who burned trash in a vacant lot. Likewise, threats
against a person because of racial or religious reasons
could cause serious trauma or start a riot—resulting in
much more "social disruption" than threats made to a person because he or she supported a particular sports team.

Because of that, Stevens said, there are "legitimate,
reasonable, and neutral" reasons to justify special rules
against hate crimes. He said that St. Paul had reason-
ably determined that the harm caused by bias-motivated
words or conduct was "qualitatively different and more
severe" than that resulting from other "fighting words."

Justice Stevens, like others involved in the case,
believed the cross burning certainly met the definition of
"fighting words," which "by their very utterance, inflict
injury." The incident—"directed as it was to a single
African American family trapped in their home—was
nothing more than a crude form of physical intimida-

tion," Stevens wrote. Nevertheless, he agreed that the St. Paul ordinance should be overturned. It was unconstitutional, Stevens said, because it was too broad and criminalized expression that was protected by the First Amendment. But, he added, if that were not the case, he would have upheld the ordinance. The ordinance, Stevens said, was "evenhanded" in its regulation of hate speech. It merely "ban[ned] punches 'below' the belt" by both sides of an issue.

Stevens said he was troubled by the majority opinion's reason for invalidating the ordinance as "an unconstitutional content-based regulation of speech." That interpretation, he said, amounted to a "near-absolute ban" on laws that limited speech by content, which would include hate-speech statutes. Such an "all-or-nothing" approach, Stevens maintained, disrupted "well-settled principles of First Amendment law." He cited several examples where the Court had allowed restrictions on speech based on content: false warranties, threats, inciting crimes, price fixing—whether a crime was committed in these cases depended on what the speaker said and the content of the message.

The justice noted that while Court-approved laws limited commercial speech by prohibiting political ads on city buses, cities could not ban hate speech under the new ruling. The majority's decision gave "fighting words" more protection than commercial speech, he said.

Whether words or expression should receive protection under the First Amendment, Stevens asserted, depended on the context in which they were uttered and the content of the speech, as well as the extent of the restrictions. So, for example, sexual words that might be protected as part of a play or a political commentary would not fall under the First Amendment's guarantee of free speech if they were uttered at a workplace to harass an employee.

REACTIONS TO DECISION

Proponents of hate-crime laws attacked the Court's ruling with scathing criticism. The majority's opinion, they contended, interfered with states' legitimate efforts to curb violent racism and protect members of minority groups from the lasting damage hate speech and crimes produce in victims. Columnist Carl Rowan blasted Scalia's opinion as "a dreadful and inflammatory decision that says to the haters and killers: 'Go ahead and burn your crosses on the private property of the people you despise; paint your swastikas on edifices of your choice; defile campuses with loud, public words of hate and hostility; we give you a constitutional shield.'" A review of the decision in the *Boston College Law Review* similarly criticized the decision, which it said signaled "a dangerous green light for those who want to intimidate and threaten members of racial, ethnic, religious and gender groups." The *Buffalo News* predicted that the "idiotic perversion of the principle of First Amendment protections" by Justice Scalia "could become a violent curse upon America."

Civil rights advocates held similar views. Kevin E. Vaughan of the Philadelphia Commission on Human Relations predicted that the ruling would have a "chilling effect" on efforts to prevent discrimination. "It makes it much more intimidating for the individual who is being harassed. Why even come forward [to complain] if the Supreme Court says it's OK?" he asked. Others called the ruling "a step back for civil rights in this country." A spokeswoman for North Carolinians Against Racist and Religious Violence said the justices "need to be educated on the history of cross burning and the history of violence directed at people's color. It's not an issue of free speech but intimidation and harassment." Tom Foley, the county attorney who defended the St. Paul ordinance in oral arguments, shared her views. "The more I read the decision, the angrier I become," he said. "I don't think that they [Supreme Court justices] knew what . . . message they were sending."

Some critics warned that the ruling would actually abridge free speech or make it difficult to determine what speech fell under First Amendment protection. Bobbie Towbin, an Anti-Defamation League official who characterized the ruling as a "disappointment," said the majority opinion presented "long-term ramifications . . . for free speech [that were] quite troubling." Editors at the *St. Petersburg* [FL] *Times* charged that Scalia and the other four justices supporting his opinion "set a precedent for savagely restricting freedom of speech" by requiring that hate-speech laws be broadened to censure all "fighting words." The editorial also questioned how the ruling would affect Florida's hate-crime law. A state judge had already issued one ruling against the law, the editorial said.

In Colorado, however, the attorney general said that his state's law was directed at "bodily harm, property destruction, or the very imminent threat of harm" and should not be affected by the decision.

Defenders of free speech and others applauded the decision as a necessary protection against censorship. In a letter to the *New York Times*, constitutional law expert Floyd Abrams described Justice Scalia's opinion as "sobering and eloquent," adding that the First Amendment is not distorted by the position "that the rules must be the same for both [sides of an issue]." He also noted that the United States is the only nation to protect vile speech as well as "civilized discourse." That fact, he observed, "is one of this country's glories, not one of its weaknesses." Another famed First Amendment scholar, Rodney Smolla, said the decision "reinforces the core of the First Amendment, which requires that government remain neutral in the marketplace of ideas." He added that the ruling sent a "ringing message that the majority of the court will hold unconstitutional virtually all government restrictions on the content of speech."

While some members of the press defended hate-crime laws and criticized Scalia's opinion, others in the news business supported the ruling. The *Washington Post*, in an editorial the day after the decision, said Americans had to preserve "a forum in which even insulting, hurtful and outrageous ideas can be expressed" as an "essential price of our system." Without such a forum, the editor concluded, "free speech would be fatally undermined."

Village Voice columnist Nat Hentoff called the decision "a startling triumph for free speech" and "a home run for the First Amendment." The New York City newspaper columnist said the ruling would extend "the range and depth of the First Amendment" and "destroy all present speech codes in public colleges and universities" as well as challenge hate-crime laws throughout the nation.

"The court has wisely identified political correctness as a danger," proclaimed an editorial in the *Houston Chronicle*. "Clearly, it is. It is inimical to the intent of the First Amendment." In California, the *Orange County Register* observed that the justices "could not rule any other way—not without incinerating the First Amendment." Edward Cleary, the attorney who represented the teen accused of cross burning, agreed: "If such laws had been in effect 30 years ago, the civil rights movement would have never gotten off the ground, because these laws make speech that creates anger in others illegal." A spokesperson for the American Civil Liberties Union expressed similar thoughts. He noted that civil rights leader Martin Luther King Jr. could have faced prosecution under the St. Paul ordinance for offending "the sensibilities of people in his own community." Other ACLU officials, however, said the organization was "very concerned about this ruling" because Scalia's opinion was "impossibly confusing" and jeopardized other, narrower hate-crime laws.

Ku Klux Klan leader Shawn Slater of Colorado praised the ruling as "the icing on the cake." He said the decision reduced the chances that police would challenge the right of his group to burn crosses as part of its ceremonies. On the opposite end of the spectrum, Ralph Washofsky, president of Temple Beth Shalom in Fort Walton Beach, Florida, also supported the decision. "My feeling is that you can't be a little bit pregnant," he said. "You either believe in free speech, or you don't."

Laura Jones, whose family was the target of the cross burning, said she hoped a new law could address the problem of hate crimes and still meet the Constitution's requirements. "I understand how we want personal rights and all that . . . but you can only go so far," she said. Her husband, Russell Jones, was less philosophical. "The

Angry residents protest a Ku Klux Klan rally held in Brownwood, Texas, on June 26, 1992. City officials, who initially opposed the Klan rally, allowed it after the U.S. Supreme Court issued its decision in *R.A.V. v. St. Paul* four days earlier, barring hate-speech laws that infringe on First Amendment rights.

people who did it will think of this as a victory," he said when asked his view of the ruling. "Basically, when these guys committed a crime, they weren't thinking about freedom of speech."

After the ruling, Foley's office announced it had dropped additional charges against Robert A. Viktora, the teen at the center of the case. Because Viktora had passed his eighteenth birthday, the prosecutor would have had to charge him as an adult. A Twin Cities paper, the Minneapolis–St.Paul *Star Tribune*, reported that a Foley aide had said the courts probably would not uphold the new charges.

A year later the Justice Department brought charges against Viktora and two of the other teens involved in the cross burning at the Joneses' home. A federal jury convicted all three of civil rights violations in connection with the incident. The U.S. Court of Appeals affirmed the convictions in 1994, ruling that the cross burnings constituted the threat of violence.

CHAPTER SIX

CENSORSHIP OR PROTECTION OF MINORITIES?

THE SUPREME COURT'S LANDMARK DECI-
sion in *R.A.V. v. St. Paul* left states, municipalities,
and public college officials scrambling to determine
whether the ruling applied to their speech codes and
hate-crime laws. Some state officials claimed that
laws that merely lengthened prison sentences for
those convicted of hate crimes would not be affected
by the new ruling. First Amendment scholars believed
otherwise. "They would have to enhance the sentence
for every crime of hate, not just racial or sexual or religious hate," said Roger Goldman, a law professor at
St. Louis University. First Amendment expert Rodney Smolla, a law professor at the College of William

and Mary, said that in his view the ruling made "almost all" the hate-crime laws unconstitutional. "The court went out of its way to enact a barrier against content-based regulation of speech that has broad implications for all of First Amendment law and goes well beyond the immediate problem it had before it."

The scholars said that Scalia's opinion could interfere with affirmative-action programs designed to compensate for years of discrimination by providing assistance to minorities. "It seems that five justices are saying there is no special need to recognize the history of discrimination," said Goldman, one of three experts who reviewed the Court's decision for the *St. Louis Post-Dispatch*.

Following the state and federal rulings, local authorities wondered whether they should continue to enforce hate-crime laws in their jurisdictions. B. W. Smith, a police captain in Fort Lauderdale, Florida, told reporters in August 1992 that his officers had a lot of questions about hate-crime law. Other officials said that witnesses to racial violence asked authorities if hate crimes were allowed under the law. "You're going to see this muddying of the waters in many situations where it doesn't apply," predicted Barbara Dougan, a Boston lawyer.

A NEW CHALLENGE

One day after the Supreme Court delivered its decision, the Wisconsin Supreme Court ruled that the state's hate-crime law violated the Constitution and struck it down. Citing the U.S. Supreme Court's ruling in *R.A.V. v. St. Paul*, the state court said the law had a chilling effect on free speech by punishing "bigoted thought," which is protected under the First Amendment. Among other provisions, the Wisconsin law had added five years in prison and a $10,000 fine for crimes motivated by bias against a person's race, national origin, religion, sexual orientation, or disability.

Attorneys for the state of Wisconsin were not happy with their high court's ruling and decided to appeal the decision to the U.S. Supreme Court. Wisconsin's case revolved around a nineteen-year-old black man named Todd Mitchell, who in 1989 led an attack on a white youth. Just before the beating, Mitchell reportedly told his friends, "There goes a white boy; go get him." The fourteen-year-old victim remained in a coma for four days as a result of the attack.

Prosecutors charged Mitchell with aggravated battery, punishable by a two-year prison sentence. The jury found Mitchell guilty of the crime and also determined that the attack had been racially motivated. Wisconsin's hate-crime law, like the statutes in more than half the other states, allowed sentences to be increased by up to five years for crimes motivated by race, religion, or other biases. With that in mind, the judge sentenced Mitchell to four years in prison. Mitchell's attorney appealed, and it was that case that resulted in the Wisconsin Supreme Court's ruling that overturned the state's hate-crime law, which had been on the books for ten years. As the case made its way to the U.S. Supreme Court, appeals courts in other states issued decisions on both sides of the controversy. The state court upheld a similar statute in Oregon, while judges struck down hate-crime legislation in Ohio and Wisconsin.

Unlike St. Paul's ordinance, which dealt only with hate crimes, Wisconsin and twenty-nine other states addressed the problem of hate crimes by increasing penalties for ordinary crimes when bias was involved. Most of the laws were based on a model statute created by the Anti-Defamation League of B'nai B'rith in the 1980s. The Supreme Court's decision to hear the Wisconsin case gave hope to those states that the ruling in *R.A.V.* might not apply to their laws. All forty-nine other states and the District of Columbia showed their support for Wisconsin's approach to hate crimes by filing a joint *amicus curiae* brief in the Supreme Court appeal. The federal government also filed an *amicus* brief for Wisconsin. In 1992 the House of Representatives had passed a bill similar to Wisconsin's law, but the Senate had rejected it. As Congress considered a new bill, the administration of President Bill Clinton supported Wisconsin's position before the Court.

Several groups that had intervened in the *R.A.V.* case

also filed *amicus* briefs in the *Wisconsin v. Mitchell* appeal. Among those filing on behalf of the Wisconsin law were U.S. Representative Charles E. Schumer, sponsor of the pending federal hate-crime bill, the City of Atlanta, several California civil rights groups, an organization representing Asian Americans, a group of state legislatures, and a number of other organizations.

In a twist that illustrated the divisions the issue had created, the national ACLU filed a brief supporting the Wisconsin law, but the Ohio branch of the organization submitted an *amicus* brief for Mitchell. The Center for Individual Rights again argued against hate-crime legislation, as did several groups of lawyers and the Wisconsin Freedom of Information Council, among others.

During oral arguments on April 21, 1993, Wisconsin attorney general James E. Doyle contended that the state statute did not "punish thought" and did not "punish the expression of any idea or belief." The law, Doyle said, punished "criminal conduct." It did not depend on "the goodness or badness" of an idea, but whether attacks motivated by that idea caused problems for the state.

He argued that it was "perfectly appropriate for the state . . . to consider [Mitchell's] reason for committing the crime in determining what the appropriate sentence should be." Careful to differentiate the Wisconsin law from the St. Paul ordinance, Doyle noted that the state had not created a new kind of crime (for example, a "hate crime") but merely increased sentences for existing crimes (assault, battery, and other criminal activity) when they were committed because of bias. "We have dealt with this strictly as a sentencing matter," Doyle said; furthermore, the additional sentencing would not apply unless the state's prosecutor had proved beyond a reasonable doubt that the crime was motivated by bias.

Deputy Solicitor General Michael R. Dreeben argued for the federal government in the case. "Government may combat discrimination in crime just as it combats discrimination in other contexts by punishing the conduct that is motivated by the race, religion, or other status of the victim," he said. Such punishment of criminal conduct did not violate the First Amendment. Instead, it served to protect citizens from harm, which is a legitimate function of federal and state governments. He argued further that if the Court discounted hatecrime provisions like Wisconsin's, the ruling would be broad enough to invalidate the nation's antidiscrimination laws, which were also based on offenders' motives.

Arguing for Mitchell, Lynn S. Adelman contended that Wisconsin's law punished thought the government found objectionable. His client's bias against white people, he said, was "crude and ugly" but "nonetheless a viewpoint." His argument met with resistance from the justices. "There are many forms of thought that are not punishable but that become punishable when translated into action," one justice observed. Adelman countered that Mitchell had already been punished for his criminal act; the added sentence punished his biased viewpoint.

The justices were not convinced. They noted that Title VII of the Civil Rights Act of 1964 punished discrimination based on race, color, religion, sex, or national origin. The Court had long ago held that antidiscrimination laws were constitutional. Adelman tried to separate the act from Mitchell's situation: "Equal opportunity," he told the Court, "is very different [from] bigotry." Depriving a person of equal opportunity—discriminating against him or her—involves an action; racism, as in Mitchell's case, is a viewpoint.

The lawyer restated his contention that the Wisconsin law required an examination of the offender's viewpoint, an action that he said violated the First Amendment. "In order to be convicted under this statute . . . it requires a biased motive, a prejudice, a belief system opposing whites." His arguments, however, failed to convince the robed questioners.

In conclusion, Adelman attempted to portray Wisconsin's hate-law provision not as a protector of minorities but as harmful to them because it stifled free expression. "More than anything minorities need an uncompromised First Amendment," he said, "for it is minorities more than anyone who are likely to think the thoughts which are offensive to the powers that be."

HATE SPEECH WORLDWIDE

America is unique in its protection of hate speech. A French court found fashion designer John Galliano guilty of hate speech in September 2011 and fined him $8,400 for having made anti-Semitic remarks to a restaurant patron and drunkenly proclaiming that he loved Hitler. The designer also lost his job at Dior, a highly regarded fashion design and retail company. In the United Kingdom three men were convicted and face a maximum sentence of seven years in prison for distributing antigay leaflets in Derby in 2011. The leaflets suggested that homosexuality should be punished by death. Similar laws in the rest of Europe criminalize speech that harms others based on their race or religion. The European Commission of Human Rights affirmed its support of hate-speech regulation as early as 1979 when it ruled that a Dutch law targeting "incitement to racial discrimination" did not violate the freedom of expression provisions of the European Convention of Human Rights.

Canada's Charter of Rights and Freedoms protects freedom of expression, but the right is not unlimited. It is a crime in Canada to intimidate, harass, attack, or threaten violence against a person, property, or group of people based on color, race, religion, ethnic origin, gender, disability, or sexual orientation. It is also illegal in Canada to incite hatred in a broadcast, over the telephone or Internet, or by other means. Canadians can make truthful statements about people or groups, and they can express a religious opinion without breaking the law. In 1990 Canada's high court let stand the sentence of a fascist who had been jailed for making hateful

Designer John Galliano was found guilty of hate speech and fined $8,400 after he proclaimed publicly in a French cafe that he loved Hitler.

telephone calls to people he was biased against. "Parliament's objective of preventing the harm caused by hate propaganda is of sufficient importance to warrant overriding a constitutional freedom," the chief justice wrote in his majority opinion. In 1996 Canada's high court affirmed that a law barring "public incitement of hatred" interfered with freedom of expression but ruled that such infringement was justified. The offender in the case was a teacher convicted of teaching anti-Semitism to his students. In 2010 two brothers who burned a cross on an interracial couple's lawn were convicted of the same charge. In 2008 Canadian courts removed two young children from a family's custody because the father taught them neo-Nazi beliefs.

In Germany, France, Romania, Poland, Israel, and Hungary, among others, it is against the law to deny that the Holocaust took place. In most of these countries a conviction carries up to five years in prison.

A judge in South Africa ruled in September 2011 that a young political leader, Julius Malema, was guilty of hate speech when he sang a freedom song from the past that included a passage urging black citizens to shoot white farmers. Under the ruling, Malema faced no criminal penalties but was obligated to pay court costs. Judge Colin Lamont, who issued the ruling, told reporters that people should focus on getting along with others in society, rather than hurting them. "The words of one person inciting others, that's how a genocide can start. No justification exists allowing the words to be sung," he said.

A resolution passed by the Council of Europe that went into effect in 2006 requires nations to make the distribution over the Internet of racist and other biased materials—including the denial of the Holocaust—a criminal offense. Sanctions apply to insults as well as threats that are motivated by race, color, national or ethnic origin, and religion. As of January 2012, twenty nations had ratified the agreement. An additional fifteen nations, including Canada, had signed the protocol but had not ratified it. The United Kingdom and Ireland are among the countries that have not signed. The United States has refused to support the resolution because it conflicts with the First Amendment's guarantee of free speech.

On June 11, 1993, Chief Justice William H. Rehnquist delivered the Court's decision in *Wisconsin v. Mitchell*. This time the Court, by another unanimous decision, upheld the hate-crime law. The opinion clarified the Court's position on hate-crime laws and supported Wisconsin's approach—and that of twenty-nine other states—of additional penalties for bias-motivated crimes. Unlike what happened in the *R.A.V.* case, the justices united behind the majority opinion in *Wisconsin v. Mitchell*. Not one concurrence was filed.

In his opinion, Chief Justice Rehnquist held that the Wisconsin law did not violate either the First Amendment or the Fourteenth Amendment, which prohibits the states from depriving citizens of their rights, including free speech. Rehnquist noted that conduct (such as burning an American flag at an antiwar rally) could sometimes express an idea and therefore fall under the protection of the First Amendment. Violent acts (like the assault in the Mitchell case), however, did not qualify for such protection "by any stretch of the imagination."

In the decision, Chief Justice Rehnquist differentiated between "motive" and "thought," a category protected by the Constitution. Under the Wisconsin law, Rehnquist said, judges could consider the motive behind an act when sentencing a person convicted of a hate-based crime. But that did not amount to a violation of free-speech rights, the chief justice said. Judges have long reviewed a number of factors, including motives, when imposing sentences—but they still have to stay within constitutional provisions. A judge who gave a severe sentence to a defendant merely because that person held "abstract beliefs," even if those beliefs were obnoxious to most other people, would have exceeded the bounds of constitutional authority. But if the convicted person's beliefs provided the motive for the crime, this circumstance would be relevant to the case and the judge could consider the motive when determining a sentence.

In addition, Rehnquist affirmed that setting penalties for crimes is a permissible role of the legislature. In this case, Wisconsin lawmakers had legitimately determined that crimes motivated by bias warranted greater penalties than other crimes. Rehnquist supported this view, stating that bias-motivated conduct was thought "to inflict greater individual and societal harm."

The chief justice likened Wisconsin's law to federal and state statutes regulating discrimination, which had already passed constitutional muster. Motive played the same role in both cases, he said. Unlike the St. Paul ordinance, which was "explicitly directed at expression," the Wisconsin law was "aimed at conduct unprotected by the First Amendment," Rehnquist said.

He concluded by dismissing Mitchell's claim that the law had a "chilling" effect on free speech because a person's previous comments could be used to prove motive. Mitchell's lawyer had suggested that a person might hesitate to express his bigoted views because he feared that if he committed a crime at some later date, his words could be used against him. Such a hypothesis, Rehnquist asserted, was "simply too speculative" to support Mitchell's argument.

State law enforcement agencies and civil rights groups applauded the decision as providing another tool to combat bigotry. Brian Levin of the Center for the Study of Ethnic and Racial Violence said he believed hate crimes could be deterred if prosecutors aggressively sought punishment for offenders under laws such as that in the Wisconsin case. The Anti-Defamation League, which wrote the model law on which the Wisconsin statute was based, asserted that the *Mitchell* decision had "largely foreclosed" additional First Amendment court challenges to enhanced sentencing for hate crimes.

Other experts, though, sharply criticized the decision. "Hate-crime laws explicitly seek to punish people for having bigoted beliefs," wrote James B. Jacobs and Kimberly Potter in their book *Hate Crimes: Criminal Law & Identity Politics*. "It would appear that the only additional purpose in punishing more severely those who commit a bias crime is to provide extra punishment based on the offender's politically incorrect opinions and viewpoints." That, they contended, would contradict the First Amendment's guarantee of free speech, adding:

"Tolerance for vile expression is the price we pay for the right to free speech."

OTHER CASES

Since its decision in *Mitchell*, the Supreme Court has ruled on several other cases involving hate speech and hate crimes. In 2000 the Court struck down a portion of a federal hate-crime law that allowed women to sue their attackers in federal court if state courts did not take action. The law, known as the Violence Against Women Act of 1994, stipulated that anyone who committed a crime of violence "motivated by gender" was liable for damages to be paid to the victim. In addressing the issue, the Court ruled in *United States v. Morrison* that the federal government has no power over criminal conduct that does not involve more than one state (as opposed to criminal activities that entail interstate commerce). The Court also ruled that the Fourteenth Amendment (which extended protection of Americans' rights to the states) did not apply when individuals (a woman's attackers, in this case) and not the state interfered with a person's civil rights. The ruling limits the role of the federal government in prosecuting hate crimes that occur outside federal jurisdiction.

In another case, *Apprendi v. New Jersey*, also decided in 2000, the Court struck down a New Jersey law that increased penalties in hate crimes. The ruling required that a jury determine "beyond a reasonable doubt" whether offenders were motivated by bias. Under the old law, a judge could make the determination.

In 2003 the Supreme Court ruled on another cross-burning case, *Virginia v. Black*, this time involving a state ban on such activities in Virginia. The Court, in another split decision, struck down the law. Justice Sandra Day O'Connor, writing for the majority, reasserted the Court's conclusion that the First Amendment protects symbolic speech—conduct that conveys a message—as well as oral and written speech. While acknowledging that a burning cross can be a powerful message of intimidation, O'Connor noted that the flaming symbol does not "inevitably convey" such a message. Historically, she said, the Ku Klux Klan used burning crosses to unify members and to convey a message of shared ideology.

The First Amendment, O'Connor said, would allow the state to ban all cross burnings "done with the intent to intimidate." However, Virginia's law also stated that all cross burnings were automatically considered to be a way to "intimidate a person or group of persons." Under that provision, state officials did not have to prove that a particular cross burning was meant to intimidate anyone. Therefore, Justice O'Connor said, the state's law was too broad, because it included in its ban instances when a burning cross was meant to express a viewpoint, protected by the First Amendment. Under the Constitution, she said, Virginia could prohibit "only those forms of intimidation that are most likely to inspire fear of bodily harm." Chief Justice William Rehquist and Justices John Paul Stevens and Stephen G. Breyer were the only ones to embrace O'Connor's entire opinion. Three other justices, Anthony M. Kennedy, Ruth Bader Ginsburg, and David H. Souter, opposed all cross-burning laws as violating the First Amendment. They joined O'Connor and the three justices supporting her opinion in ruling that the Virginia law was unconstitutional.

Justices Clarence Thomas and Antonin Scalia dissented and supported the Virginia law, although Scalia agreed with O'Connor that the judge had improperly instructed the jury at the trial of Barry E. Black and for that reason his conviction should be overturned and the case retried. Justice Thomas, the Court's only African American member, contended that cross burning by its very nature—and because of its historical association with racial violence—should be considered an act of terrorism not protected by the First Amendment. The Virginia law, he said, dealt with conduct, not expression. A number of civil rights leaders, law enforcement officials, and others endorsed Thomas's view of cross burnings.

STATE AND FEDERAL LAWS TODAY

Today hate-crime laws are on the books in all states but Wyoming. Forty-five states have laws with special provisions for crimes motivated by ethnicity, race, and religion. Thirty-one states recognize gender and thirty include disability as protected categories. Laws in twenty-seven states have added sexual orientation, fourteen states include age, and seven have placed political affiliation on the list of special classes that receive protection under hate-crime legislation.

In 2009 President Barack Obama signed into law an act of Congress that expands the circumstances in which penalties for hate crimes could apply, including the addition of gender identity and sexual orientation to the list of biases. The law applies to perceived as well as actual bias. For example, if a gang attacked a person they mistakenly thought was gay, the act would still be considered a hate crime because it was motivated by homophobia.

The new measure was named in honor of Matthew Shepard and James Byrd Jr. Shepard, a gay twenty-one-year-old college student in Wyoming, died in October 1998 after two men, who had kidnapped and beaten him, left him tied to a split-rail fence. Byrd, an African American, died in June of that year after members of a white supremacist group in Texas chained him to a truck and dragged him for three miles along a logging road. The new law expanded the reach of the federal government, allowing federal agents to prosecute as hate crimes violations that states have failed to prosecute.

Based on statistics compiled by the Federal Bureau

Judy Shepard (*left*), mother of Matthew Shepard, and Betty Byrd Boatner (*center*), James Byrd's sister, pose with President Barack Obama after the signing of the Matthew Shepard and James Byrd Jr. Hate Crimes Prevention Act in 2009.

of Investigation (FBI), 6,628 hate crimes were reported in 2010 (the most recent report available). Nearly half of those incidents were motivated by racial bias (47.3 percent), and most of those (69.8 percent) were committed against African Americans. More than 19 percent of hate crimes reported in 2010 targeted victims based on their sexual orientation (almost all attacks were antigay). Twenty percent of the reported hate crimes involved religion, and 65.4 percent of those were against Jews. Almost 13 percent affected people based on their ethnicity or national origin, with 65.5 percent aimed at Hispanics. Disability accounted for 0.6 percent (46 offenses) of the bias behind reported hate crimes—24 offenses because of bias against mental illness and 22 against physical disability. The FBI figures include only those hate crimes reported to the police.

Other sources say the FBI's figures underreport the true number of hate crimes. The Southern Poverty Law Center, a civil rights group based in Alabama, estimates that victims report only about one-fifth of the hate crimes actually committed. The federal Bureau of Justice Statistics (BJS) has used data from many sources to arrive at much larger numbers of hate crimes, many of which are never reported to police. The bureau estimates that 148,400 hate crimes occurred in 2009, a decrease of about 38 percent from the 239,400 incidents identified by BJS in 2003. "In many cases, hate may be seen or perceived by the victims, their families, witnesses and even law enforcement to be the motivation for a crime, but perpetrators may not be charged with a hate crime for a variety of reasons," wrote the authors of a 2007 report on hate crimes produced for the Department of Justice.

WHEN IS A CRIME A "HATE CRIME"?

The wide discrepancies in the number of hate crimes identified by different agencies reflect the ambiguity surrounding the issue. Part of the problem lies in the difficulty in determining whether an act is a hate crime. Depending on the jurisdiction where the act was committed, the label "hate crime" may apply only to harassment or to murder. The model law prepared by the Anti-Defamation League and adopted by many states focuses on harassment and intimidation. The Washington, D.C., law uses the hate-crime label for more serious offenses, such as aggravated assault, arson, and murder. The state of Alabama adopted a hate-crime law that applies to all offenses—misdemeanors and felonies—motivated by race, religion, and other specified biases.

Another example, posed by legal experts Jacobs and Potter, involved an African American man who targeted white people for robberies because he believed they were wealthier than members of other races. The robber's choice was not inspired by hatred or bigotry, but it did depend on race. He would have been guilty of a hate crime in some states but not in others that require police to prove that prejudice motivated the crime.

One tragic case that illustrates the problems with hate-crime laws is that of Tyler Clementi, a Rutgers University first-year student who committed suicide in September 2010 after a tape of Clementi having a sexual encounter with a man was broadcast over the Internet. Many considered the taping a hate crime. New Jersey officials accused Clementi's roommate, Dharun Ravi, of taping and broadcasting the encounter and charged Ravi with bias intimidation (committing a hate crime) among other violations. The charge carries a sentence of up to ten years in prison. In December 2011 Ravi rejected a

Former Rutgers student Dharun Ravi in Middlesex County Court during a hearing in September 2011.

plea agreement with prosecutors that promised no jail time and opted to go to trial. The jury found Ravi guilty on all counts on March 16, 2012. A week later Ravi said he would appeal the conviction.

At least one expert in the field questioned whether Ravi's actions really qualified as a hate crime. Marc Poirier, a Seton Hall Law School professor, noted that Ravi had taunted and embarrassed Clementi, but he had not attacked him physically. Most hate crimes are associated with violence of some kind. The incident did not involve "physical or threatened violence," he said. "It's two roommates who don't get along." One way to avoid such encounters, Poirier said, is to revise the roommate system to limit friction between students, as Rutgers and other schools are doing.

Poirier said New Jersey dealt with the matter appropriately when it passed a strong antibullying law almost immediately after Clementi's suicide. The new statute requires the state's public schools to adopt a comprehensive antibullying program that includes training for teachers and students, safety teams to monitor schools for bullying, and quick investigations of bullying reports. Critics of the new law, however, observe that it may run into the same problems faced by college speech codes if schools are required to police harsh language.

SPEECH CODES ON TRIAL

Hundreds of college campuses have their own hate-speech policies, or codes of conduct that include provisions on hate speech. Some follow the model of the Wisconsin law that the Supreme Court affirmed in 1993. Others, however, clearly challenge free-speech principles. Timothy C. Shiell, in his 2009 book *Campus Hate Speech on Trial*, reports that courts have ruled unconstitutional every college hate-speech code that has come before them.

In one of the early cases challenging a college hate-speech code, a psychology graduate student (referred to as John Doe in court) sued the University of Michigan in 1989 on the grounds that its policy unconstitutionally interfered with his free speech. Doe feared that he would run afoul of the university code when he discussed certain theories involving biological differences between men and women and between races. Striking down the school's speech code, district court judge Avern Cohn stated, "While the Court is sympathetic to the University's obligation to ensure equal educational opportunities for all of its students, such efforts must not be at the expense of free speech." Citing several Supreme Court decisions, he noted that under certain circumstances speech could be restricted, but the university could not ban speech just because it was offensive or because officials disagreed with the ideas or messages conveyed. "These principles," the judge added, "acquire a special significance in the University setting, where the free and unfettered interplay of competing views is essential to the institution's educational mission."

Several other court decisions on college speech codes affirmed the *Doe* ruling and reiterated the First Amendment's guarantee of free expression. In each, the court ruled that universities could punish speech only under strictly defined circumstances. The code or policy

- had to be narrow enough so that every student knew exactly what was banned;
- could not ban speech or expression protected under the First Amendment;
- could not punish words or expression based on officials' objection to its content or message;

• had to serve a state's "compelling interest" that could be accomplished only through the code.

The University of Wisconsin's code relied on the "fighting words" doctrine established in *Chaplinsky v. New Hampshire*. In a 1991 decision, however, the district court found that the code violated the Constitution. Under the code, officials could censure words that were hostile, intimidating, or demeaning. But, the Court concluded, that was not enough to meet First Amendment requirements that words could be banned only if they "tend[ed] to incite violence."

Other decisions threw out official sanctions against a fraternity spoof, which university authorities said demeaned women and black Americans; ruled in favor of a coach whose contract was not renewed after he used the word "nigger"; and struck down Stanford University's speech code on grounds that it violated the First Amendment. The Supreme Court decision in *R.A.V. v. St. Paul* bolstered the courts' commitment to requiring that college speech codes not violate constitutional protections.

A more recent decision involving university speech codes, delivered by the U.S. Court of Appeals in 2010, addressed the constitutionality of the University of the Virgin Islands code of conduct provisions on speech and expression. The court ruled that the code was too broad; covered speech protected by the First Amendment, including speech that was merely "offensive"; and undermined the "critical importance" of free speech on college campuses.

The decision also pronounced that college officials did not "hold the same power over students" that public elementary and high school authorities did. "Modern day public universities," the court wrote, "are intended to function as marketplaces of ideas, where students interact with each other and with their professors in a collaborative learning environment," which might include views and values not embraced by the college. Undercutting one of the major justifications colleges used in establishing codes of conduct and speech, the court ruled that universities cannot act as parents when setting rules; they must treat their students as adults.

Free-speech proponents, conservative Christians, and others applauded the ruling. Christian groups have objected to campus speech policies because of concern that statements against homosexuality, feminism, and other sensitive topics, made in accordance with religious beliefs, would be considered "offensive" by college officials and punished. "Christian students shouldn't have to fear censorship by university officials simply for expressing their beliefs," said Casey Mattox, an attorney for Alliance Defense Fund, a legal group representing conservative Christian interests.

Critics of speech codes on campus argue that the

David French, president of the Foundation for Individual Rights in Education (FIRE), discusses the group's free speech advocacy work at the organization's headquarters in Philadelphia. FIRE aims to ensure that colleges respect the free speech rights of students and faculty members on their campuses.

best way to fight discrimination and bigotry is to expose these attitudes and bring them to the light, where they can be knocked down through reasoned debate. "Universities should confront offensive ideas by rebuttal, not by suppression," says Martin Gruberg, political science professor at the University of Wisconsin. "John Milton, John Stuart Mill, and Oliver Wendell Holmes had it right: truth doesn't need a stacked deck to be victorious."

Despite the setbacks in court, many colleges continue to promulgate speech codes. "It is false (a myth) to say that universities are reluctant to punish student speech," says Thor Halvorssen, executive director of the

Foundation for Individual Rights in Education (FIRE), a nonprofit group working for free speech on college campuses. "Colleges and universities routinely punish students and faculty for their speech, their writing, and even their membership in campus groups." In its 2011 report, the group maintained that 67 percent of the 390 colleges in its survey have speech codes or other policies that "seriously infringe" on students' freedom of speech.

University officials say their policies aim to encourage respectful debate, not to censor speech. "What we attempt to do is try to create a civil democracy, where everybody is respected," says Anthony Ceddia, president of Shippensburg University. The Pennsylvania school received a "green light" in FIRE's 2011 and 2012 reports, awarded to colleges whose policies do not seriously threaten free speech.

HATE SPEECH AND THE INTERNET

Hate speech distributed over the Internet presents a particular challenge to law enforcement officials and others trying to curtail its spread. These professionals fear that hate speech on the Internet may encourage mentally disturbed people to take violent action against the government or certain groups. Video clips posted in December 2010 on the Internet by Jared L. Loughner, accused in the January 2011 shooting of Representative Gabrielle Giffords, a federal judge, and others in Arizona, spurred concerns over the influence of vitriolic rhetoric on the Internet. Loughner's words mimicked words posted on sites maintained by various extremist groups, officials said. "The ubiquitous nature of the Internet means that not only threats but also hate speech and other inciteful speech is much more readily available to individuals than quite clearly it was 8 or 10 or 15 years ago," says FBI director Robert S. Mueller III. "That absolutely presents a challenge for us, particularly when it results in what would be lone wolves or lone offenders undertaking attacks."

Those pushing for controls on hate speech on the Internet compare the hatemongering on blogs, social networking sites, and websites to the Nazis' hate-filled propaganda against the Jews in the 1930s and 1940s, which escalated into the Holocaust. These observers fear such venom will incite acts of violence, either in those spewing the hateful words or in others. International groups have passed several resolutions aimed at controlling widespread distribution of hate speech over the Internet. In its protocol requiring nations to prohibit Internet hate speech, the Council of Europe states: "[N]ational and international law need to provide adequate legal responses to propaganda of a racist and xenophobic nature committed through computer systems."

The Simon Wiesenthal Center, a Jewish human rights organization, identified ten thousand websites that

Congresswoman Gabrielle Giffords waves at people attending a one-year anniversary vigil commemorating the victims and survivors of the shooting spree that nearly cost the Arizona representative her life.

spread extremist or terrorist views in 2009. The organization works with Facebook and other social networks to remove such material, which violates users' agreements to abide by the sites' terms of service. However, the Wiesenthal Center noted in 2009 that efforts to remove hate speech had not kept up with the influx of new material. France, Germany, and Italy, among others, have ordered Yahoo Groups and other hosts of Internet forums to prevent their members from viewing denials of the Holocaust and other examples of material considered to be hate speech.

Free-speech advocates argue that efforts to rid the Internet of hate speech are ineffective and ultimately doomed to failure. Laws against hate speech distributed over the Internet are "entirely *inadequate* for this purpose," says Sandy Starr, an expert on Internet regulation. Pressure on Internet service providers and video-sharing websites such as YouTube may remove some offensive material, but new sites quickly replace those that are shut down. Proponents of free speech believe that a better way of dealing with hate speech, on the Internet or otherwise, is to combat it with education and debate. By criminalizing opinions that preach hate, Starr contends, officials "inadvertently bolster them, by removing them from the far more effective and democratic mechanism of public scrutiny and political debate."

HATE SPEECH REGULATIONS: EFFECTIVE OR NOT?

Proponents of categorizing hate crimes differently from other crimes argue that harsher penalties help to deter acts motivated by prejudice. Hate-crime laws are needed, they say, to quell what has become a growing problem in American society. "A strong prison sentence sends a signal to would-be hatemongers everywhere that should they illegally express their bigotry, they can expect to receive more than a mere slap on the wrist," say sociologists Jack Levin and Jack McDevitt. Advocates also note that members of groups that have been victimized in the past can take comfort in knowing that the community stands behind them and that hate-crime offenders will be severely punished under hate-crime laws.

Critics of hate-crime laws maintain that all crimes are hateful, and it serves no purpose to establish different treatments for those motivated by certain biases. There is no evidence, they say, that hate-crime laws reduce bias among criminals. In their book on hate crimes, Jacobs and Potter say there is no evidence of an epidemic in hate crimes, only an increase in the use of the label. On the whole, they maintain, society is more tolerant and less biased than in centuries past—not because of hate-crime laws but because of a change in society's attitudes toward discrimination and prejudice. They point to the treatment of American Indians and the acceptance of slavery and lynchings as examples of a past that saw much more violence against minorities.

In their argument against the hate-crime label, Jacobs and Potter contend that existing laws are more than adequate to punish those who commit hate crimes. "There is no reason to believe," they say, "that prejudice-motivated offenders, particularly those who commit violent crimes, were not or could not be punished severely enough under generic criminal laws." They believe that enhancing sentences for bias-motivated murder makes little sense when states already punish the crime with the death penalty or life in prison. Worse, they say, the special treatment given to bias-motivated crimes divides Americans into groups and puts emphasis on one type of crime while diverting attention from crime in general. Jacobs and Potter also dispute the position that victims of bias-induced crime suffer to a greater degree than other victims. All crime victims suffer, they note, some physically, some psychologically as well, depending on the nature of the crime.

The verdict is still out on the effectiveness of hate-crime laws and whether they achieve the goals proponents have used to justify them. But whether hate-crime laws serve a useful purpose or not, the Supreme Court's ruling in *R.A.V.* stands as a stern warning to states and municipalities not to violate Americans' rights in their enforcement of such statutes. The First Amendment stands as a barrier to protect the right to express oneself from laws that infringe against free speech—even when that expression is hateful and hurtful.

In his eloquent dissent in a 1929 case, Supreme Court Justice Oliver Wendell Holmes Jr. reminded citizens of the meaning of the First Amendment's guarantee of free speech, protection that applied even to vile, hostile words: "[I]f there is any principle of the Constitution that more imperatively calls for attachment than any other it is the principle of free thought—not free thought for those who agree with us but freedom for the thought that we hate."

THE FIRST AMENDMENT

GUARDIAN OF FUNDAMENTAL RIGHTS

After the American Revolution, citizens set out to create a government for their new nation that would not duplicate Britain's abuses of power that led to war. The Constitution they adopted established a blueprint for the government's operations, while the Bill of Rights protected individual rights from interference by a powerful federal government.

Number one on the Bill of Rights, the First Amendment, guarantees individual Americans some of their most precious rights:

- Freedom to practice their own religious beliefs and a ban on a state religion that would receive preferential treatment over other faiths.
- Freedom to speak without fear of punishment by the government for expressing their views.
- Freedom for the press to publish without interference from the government.
- Freedom to meet in a peaceful manner and associate with whomever they choose.
- Freedom to protest against government actions and to join together to demand change.

121

In drafting the First Amendment, the founders recognized several principles of American democracy:

- People have a right to freedom (although black Americans were not granted this right until the Thirteenth Amendment abolished slavery).
- Democracy relies on the free expression of its citizenry. To make informed choices about government and their leaders, citizens must have access to a free flow of information. A free "marketplace of ideas" provides citizens with a variety of views and facts on which to evaluate candidates for public office and to assess their performance. Such freedom cannot exist if the government controls the information Americans are allowed to receive.
- The government (and Congress's laws) must not interfere with Americans' basic rights. However, the courts have allowed government to regulate fundamental rights, including freedom of speech, under certain circumstances.
- When rights conflict with each other, the courts must balance them to determine which one has priority. For example, extensive media coverage (freedom of the press) may have an impact on a person's right to a fair trial.
- The First Amendment applies to everyone. Americans are entitled to express their opinions or follow their religion even when other people find such views or religious practices to be offensive.

Since its ratification on December 15, 1791, the First Amendment has stood between Americans and attempts by overzealous moralists, self-promoting politicians, and overreaching officials to stifle dissent, muffle the media, intimidate members of unpopular groups, quell protests, and impose religious views on people whose beliefs are at odds with the majority. The First Amendment has been at the heart of dozens of U.S. Supreme Court cases involving religion or individual beliefs, protest, free speech, and freedom of the press.

The First Amendment often lies at the center of bitter disputes. Despite its lead position in the Bill of Rights, the First Amendment—or at least its interpretation by the courts—has frequently given rise to howls of protest. Does the guarantee of free speech apply to protesters who express their views by burning the flag? Does freedom of the press extend to pornographic magazines and films? Does freedom of religion mean that children cannot sing Christmas carols in public schools? The answers to those questions are not always clear, and court decisions in cases that arise from them are often controversial and unpopular.

Yet that is how a democracy operates. Disputes rage, courts issue rulings, and people use their First Amendment right to free speech to applaud or denigrate the results. It's a free country—in large part because of the protections that the First Amendment provides.

NOTES

INTRODUCTION

p. 8, "The Order believed . . .": Howard Pankratz, "Neo-Nazi Gunman in Alan Berg's Murder Dies in Prison," *Denver Post*, August 17, 2010, www.denverpost.com/news/ci_15805243

p. 8, "At the trial, . . .": Pankratz, "Neo-Nazi Gunman in Alan Berg's Murder Dies in Prison."

pp. 9–10, "If the skulls . . .": John Leo, "The Politics of Hate," *U.S. News & World Report*, October 9, 1989, 24; cited in James B. Jacobs and Kimberly Potter, *Hate Crimes: Criminal Law & Identity Politics* (New York: Oxford University Press, 1998), 4.

CHAPTER ONE

p. 16, "I wonder . . .": Conrad deFiebre, "Burning Cross Greets Black Family on St. Paul's East Side," *Star Tribune* [Minnneapolis–St. Paul], June 22, 1990, 1.

p. 16, "The Police Department . . .": deFiebre, "Burning Cross Greets Black Family on St. Paul's East Side."

p. 19, "The city wanted . . .": Paul Gustafson, "High Court Will Review St. Paul Hate Crime Law," *Star Tribune* [Minneapolis–St. Paul], June 11, 1991, 1.

pp. 20–21, "Hate crime assault. . .": Larry Tye, "Hate Crimes on Rise in US Racial Attacks, Gay Bashing Burgeoning," *Boston Globe*, July 29, 1990, 1.

p. 21, "There is no . . .": Tye, "Hate Crimes on Rise in US Racial Attacks, Gay Bashing Burgeoning."

CHAPTER TWO

p. 30, "He said the flag . . .": Edward J. Cleary, *Beyond the Burning Cross* (New York: Vintage Books, 1994), 38.

p. 31, "Cross burning . . .": Paul Gustafson and Anthony Lonetree, "Judge Tosses Out Part of Cross Burning Ordinance," *Star Tribune* [Minneapolis–St. Paul], July 18, 1990, 1.

p. 32, "Instead, the justices . . .": Cleary, *Beyond the Burning Cross*, 56–58.

p. 32, "Burning a cross . . .": *In the Matter of the Welfare of R.A.V.*, *Supreme Court of Minnesota*, 464 N.W.2d 507 (1991).

CHAPTER THREE

p. 39, "The First Amendment . . .": Edward J. Cleary, *Beyond the Burning Cross* (New York: Vintage Books, 1994), 64.

p. 40, The city ordinance, . . .": Petitioner's Brief, *R.A.V. v. St. Paul*, 505 US 377 (1992).

p. 40, "Clearly there . . .": Petitioner's Brief, *R.A.V. v. St. Paul*, 505 US 377 (1992).

p. 42, "Burning a cross . . .": Tony Mauro, "Issue of Cross Burning: A Right? Or a Wrong?" *USA Today*, June 11, 1991, 8.

p. 42, "I would hope . . .": Linda Greenlaw, "Justices to Decide If Hate-Crime Law Illegally Curbs Freedom of Expression," *New York Times*, June 11, 1991, www.nytimes.com/1991/06/11/us/supreme-court-roundup-justices-decide-if-hate-crime-law-illegally-curbs-freedom.html

p. 43, "The crime . . .": Mauro, "Issue of Cross Burning: A Right? Or a Wrong?"

p. 44, "Hate speech, . . .": Ryan Heman, "More Speech, not Less, and Certainly not Hate Speech," *Tufts Daily*, February 15, 2011, www.tuftsdaily.com/op-ed/more-speech-not-less-and-certainly-not-hate-speech-1.2469200?pagereq=1

p. 45, "Universities ought . . .": "Hate Speech on Campus," American Civil Liberties Union, www.aclu.org/free-speech/hate-speech-campus

p. 45, "After a student . . .": "About Project Civility," Rutgers University website, http://projectcivility.rutgers.edu/about-project-civility

p. 45, "At Arizona State . . .": "Campus Environment Team," Arizona State University, https://provost.asu.edu/index.php?q=cet/

p. 46, "I think the case . . .": Scott Lanman, "Jacobowitz Settles 'Water Buffalo' Lawsuit," *Daily Pennsylvanian*, September 8, 1997, http://thedp.com/index.php/article/1997/09/jacobowitz_settles_water_buffalo_lawsuit

p. 46, "Hate speech, . . .": Alexander Tsesis, "Burning Crosses on Campus: University Hate Speech Codes," *Connecticut Law Review*, 43:2 (December 2010), http://rsa.cwrl.utexas.edu/node/4473

p. 47, "The First Amendment . . .": Tamar Lewin, "Hate-Crime Law Is Focus of Case on Free Speech," *New York Times*, December 1, 1991, www.nytimes.com/1991/12/01/us/hate-crime-law-is-focus-of-case-on-free-speech.html

p. 48, "In the play . . .": Robert Bolt, *A Man for All Seasons* (New York: Samuel French Inc., 1990), 56.

p. 48, "The result . . .": Edward Cleary, brief for petitioner, *R.A.V. v. St. Paul*. Cited in Ronald K. L. Collins and Sam Chaltain, *We Must Not Be Afraid to Be Free: Stories of Free Expression in America* (New York: Oxford University Press, 2011), 190.

p. 49, "Second, the lawyers . . .": Tom Foley, brief for respondent, *R.A.V. v. St. Paul.* Cited in Andrea L. Crowley, "*R.A.V. v. City of St. Paul*: How the Supreme Court Missed the Writing on the Wall," *Boston College Law Review,* 34:4:4 (1993), 790–791.

p. 52, "Our whole constitutional . . .": *Stanley v. Georgia,* 394 U.S. 557 (1969).

CHAPTER FOUR

pp. 56–65, Oral Arguments, *R.A.V. v. St. Paul,* 505 U.S. 377 (1992).

CHAPTER FIVE

p. 71, "For example, . . .": Antonin Scalia and Kevin A. Ring, *Scalia Dissents: Writings of the Supreme Court's Wittiest, Most Outspoken Justice* (Washington, DC: Regnery Publishing, 2004), 108–112.

p. 71, "In a 1996 . . .": Scalia and Ring, *Scalia Dissents,* ix.

p. 71, "He once derided . . .": "Scalia and Ring, *Scalia Dissents,* 41.

p. 71, "Ruth Bader Ginsburg's . . .": *United States v. Virginia et al.,* 518 U.S. 515 (1996).

p. 72, "Two hunters . . .": Dahlia Lithwick, "The Steve and Nino Show," *Slate,* October 6, 2011, www.slate.com/articles/news_ and_politics/jurisprudence/2011/10/breyer_and_scalia_ unintentionally_make_the_case_for_cameras_in_t.html

p. 72, "I just have . . .": Lithwick, "The Steve and Nino Show."

p. 72, "He plays . . .": Adam Liptak, "So, Guy Walks Up to the Bar, and Scalia Says . . . ," *New York Times,* December 31, 2005, www. nytimes.com/2005/12/31/politics/31mirth.html?scp=1&sq= scalia%20funniest%20justice&st=cse

p. 82, "Columnist Carl Rowan . . .": Carl T. Rowan, "Court Encourages Haters and Killers," syndicated column, June 26, 1992, 35.

pp. 82–83, "A review . . .": Andrea L. Crowley, "*R.A.V. v. City of St. Paul*: How the Supreme Court Missed the Writing on the Wall," *Boston College Law Review,* 34:4:4 (July 1, 1993), 801.

p. 83, "The *Buffalo News* . . .": Editorial, "Scalia and Pals Give Hatred a Hand," *Buffalo* [NY] *News,* June 29, 1992, B3.

p. 83, "Kevin E. Vaughn . . .": Aaron Epstein, "High Court Voids Ban on Hate Crimes," *Philadelphia Inquirer,* June 23, 1992, 1.

p. 83, "Others called . . .": James H. Rubin, "Justices Kill Hate Crimes Ordinance," *Morning Call* [Allentown, PA], June 23, 1992, 1.

p. 83, "A spokeswoman . . .": Rubin, "Justices Kill Hate Crimes Ordinance."

p. 83, "The more I . . .": Gustafson, "Hate-Crime Ordinance Rejected: St. Paul Measure Limited Free Speech, Court Says," *Star Tribune* [Minneapolis–St. Paul], June 23, 1992, 1.

p. 83, "Bobbie Towbin, . . .": Peter G. Chronis, "State Law Expected to Survive," *Denver Post*, June 23, 1992, 1.

p. 84, "Editors at the . . .": Editorial, "A Dangerous Precedent," *St. Petersburg* [FL] *Times*, June 24, 1992, 10.

p. 84, "In Colorado, . . .": Chronis, "State Law Expected to Survive."

p. 84, "In a letter . . .": Floyd Abrams, "Right Way to Read 'Hate Speech' Opinion," *New York Times*, July 3, 1992, 24.

p. 84, "Another famed . . .": Epstein, "High Court Voids Ban on Hate Crimes."

p. 85, "The *Washington Post*, . . .": Nat Hentoff, "A Startling Triumph for Free Speech," *Village Voice*, July 28, 1992, 18.

p. 85, "The court has wisely . . .": Editorial, "Hate Crimes: Court Rightly Identifies Political Correctness Dangers," *Houston Chronicle*, June 23, 1992, 14.

p. 85, "In California, . . .": Editorial, "Crossing Free Speech's Line," *Orange County Register* [Santa Ana, CA], June 23, 1992, 10.

p. 85, "Edward Cleary, . . .": Gustafson, "Hate-Crime Ordinance Rejected: St. Paul Measure Limited Free Speech, Court Says."

p. 86, "He noted . . .": Rubin, "Justices Kill Hate Crimes Ordinance."

p. 86, "Other ACLU . . .": Tom Hamburger, "Hate-Crime Ordinance Rejected: Moves to Fight Bias Crimes Thrown into Doubt by Ruling," *Star Tribune* [Minneapolis–St. Paul], June 23, 1992, 1.

p. 86, "Ku Klux Klan . . .": Chronis, "State Law Expected to Survive."

p. 86, "My feeling . . .": Editorial, "High Court's 'Hate' Decision," *Northwest Florida Daily News*, June 24, 1992, 4A.

p. 86, "I understand . . .": Dick Lehr, "High Court Overturns 'Hate Crime' Ordinance," *Boston Globe*, June 23, 1992, 1.

pp. 86–87, "The people . . .": Gustafson, "Hate-Crime Ordinance Rejected: St. Paul Measure Limited Free Speech, Court Says."

CHAPTER SIX

p. 89, "They would . . .": "Ruling Aimed at Hate-Speech Laws, Scholars Say," *St. Louis Post-Dispatch*, June 24, 1992, 1C.

p. 90, "The court went . . .": Ruth Marcus, "Supreme Court Overturns Law Barring Hate Crimes," *Washington Post*, June 23, 1992, 1.

p. 90, "It seems . . .": "Ruling Aimed at Hate-Speech Laws, Scholars Say."

p. 90, "You're going to . . .": Katia Hetter, "Enforcers of Hate-Crime Laws Wary after High Court Ruling," *Wall Street Journal*, August 13, 1992, 1.

p. 91, "Citing the U.S. . . .": "The Supreme Court: Wisconsin Court Overturns Stiffer Terms for Hate Crimes," *New York Times*, June 25, 1992, 10.

p. 91, "There goes a white boy, . . .": *Wisconsin v. Mitchell*, 508 U.S. 476 (1993).

p. 93, "During oral arguments . . .": Oral Arguments, *Wisconsin v. Mitchell*, 508 U.S. 476 (1993).

p. 94, "Government may combat . . .": Oral Arguments, *Wisconsin v. Mitchell*, 508 U.S. 476 (1993).

p. 94, "His client's bias . . .": Oral Arguments, *Wisconsin v. Mitchell*, 508 U.S. 476 (1993).

pp. 94–95, "There are many . . .": Oral Arguments, *Wisconsin v. Mitchell*, 508 U.S. 476 (1993).

p. 95, "Equal opportunity, . . .": Oral Arguments, *Wisconsin v. Mitchell*, 508 U.S. 476 (1993).

p. 95, "In order to be . . .": Oral Arguments, *Wisconsin v. Mitchell*, 508 U.S. 476 (1993).

p. 95, "More than anything . . .": Oral Arguments, *Wisconsin v. Mitchell*, 508 U.S. 476 (1993).

p. 96, "The European Commission . . .": David Pannick, "Smother Hate with Freedom of Speech," *Times* [London, UK], July 28, 1992.

p. 97, "Parliament's objective . . .": "When Is It Hate Speech?: 7 Significant Canadian Cases," CBC News, October 12, 2011, www.cbc.ca/news/canada/story/2011/10/12/f-free-speech-hate-crimes.html

p. 98, "The words . . .": Alan Cowell, "A.N.C. Official Convicted of Hate Speech," *New York Times*, September 13, 2011, A8.

p. 101, "The Anti-Defamation . . .": "Hate Crime Laws," Anti-Defamation League, www.adl.org/99hatecrime/constitutionality.asp

p. 101, "Hate-crime laws . . .": James B. Jacobs and Kimberly Potter, *Hate Crimes: Criminal Law & Identity Politics* (New York: Oxford University Press, 1998), 126–128.

pp. 102–103, "The ruling . . .": *Apprendi v. New Jersey*, 530 U.S. 466 (2000).

p. 107, "In many cases, . . .": Michael Shively and Carrie F. Mulford, "Hate Crime in America: The Debate Continues," *NIJ Journal*, no. 257, June 2007.

p. 109, "The incident . . .": "Examining the Bias Charge in the Tyler Clementi Case," *Star-Ledger* [NJ], September 11, 2011, http://blog.nj.com/njv_editorial_page/2011/09/examining_the_bias_charge_in_t.html

p. 111, "While the Court . . .": *Doe v. University of Michigan*, No. 89-71683, 721 F. Supp. 852 (E.D. Mich. 1989).

p. 112, "But, the Court . . .": Timothy C. Shiell, *Campus Hate Speech on Trial*, 2nd ed. (Lawrence: University Press of Kansas, 2009), 76–79.

p. 112, "The court ruled . . .": *McCauley v. University of the Virgin Islands*, 618F. 3d 232, Court of Appeals, 3rd Circuit, 2010.

p. 113, "Christian students . . .": "New Court Decision Reinforces Need for Speech Policy Changes at Five Colleges, Universities," Alliance Defense Fund press release, August 26, 2010, www.adfmedia.org/News/PRDetail/4315?

pp. 113–114, "Universities should confront . . .": Shiell, *Campus Hate Speech on Trial*, 141.

p. 114, "It is false . . .": David L. Hudson Jr., "Hate Speech & Campus Speech Codes," First Amendment Center, www.firstamendmentcenter.org/hate-speech-campus-speech-codes

p. 115, "In its 2011 . . .": "Spotlight on Speech Codes 2011: The State of Free Speech on Our Nation's Campuses," Foundation for Individual Rights in Education, 2011.

p. 115, "What we attempt . . .": Mary Beth Marklein, "On Campus: Free Speech for You but not for Me?" *USA Today*, November 3, 2003, www.usatoday.com/news/washington/2003-11-02-free-speech-cover_x.htm

p. 116, "The ubiquitous . . .": Kirk Johnson, Serge F. Kovaleski, Dan Frosch, and Eric Lipton, "Suspect's Odd Behavior Caused Growing Alarm," *New York Times*, January 10, 2011, A1.

p. 116, "[N]ational and . . .": "Additional Protocol to the Convention on Cybercrime," Convention Committee on Cybercrime, January 28, 2003, http://conventions.coe.int/Treaty/en/Treaties/html/189.htm

p. 118, "Laws against hate . . .": Sandy Starr, "Hate Speech: What Is There to Be Worried About?" Presentation to the OSCE conference on Guaranteeing Media Freedom on the Internet, Amsterdam, August 27, 2004, www.osce.org/fom/36098

p. 118, "A strong prison . . .": Jack Levin and Jack McDevitt, *Hate Crimes: The Rising Tide of Bigotry & Bloodshed* (New York: Plenum Press, 1993), 179; cited in Jacobs and Potter, 89.

p. 119, "There is no . . .": Jacobs and Potter, 65.

p. 120, "[I]f there is . . .": Oliver Wendell Holmes, Dissent, *United States v. Schwimmer*, 279 U.S. 644 (1929).

FURTHER INFORMATION

AUDIO/VIDEO

Garbus, Liz, dir. *Shouting Fire: Stories From the Edge of Free Speech.* HBO, 2009, DVD.

Hegedus, Chris. *The First Amendment Project.* Sundance Channel Home Entertainment, 2005, DVD.

BOOKS

Fridell, Ron. *U.S. v. Eichman: Flag Burning and Free Speech.* New York: Marshall Cavendish, 2008.

Gold, Susan Dudley. *Tinker v. Des Moines: Free Speech for Students.* New York: Marshall Cavendish Benchmark, 2007.

Jacobs, Thomas A. *Teen Cyberbullying Investigated: Where Do Your Rights End and Consequences Begin?* Minneapolis: Free Spirit Publishing, 2010.

Johnson, John W., and Robert P. Green Jr. *Affirmative Action.* Santa Barbara, CA: Greenwood Press, 2009.

Lamb, Brian, Susan Swain, and Mark Farkas, eds. *The Supreme Court.* New York: PublicAffairs, 2010.

Lentin, Alana. *Racism and Ethnic Discrimination.* New York: Rosen Publishing Group, 2011.

Lewis, Anthony. *Freedom for the Thought That We Hate: A Biography of the First Amendment.* New York: Basic Books, 2008.

Patrick, John J. *The Supreme Court of the United States: A Student Companion.* New York: Oxford University Press, USA, 2006.

Pederson, Charles E. *Racism and Intolerance.* Yankton, SD: Erickson Press, 2008.

WEBSITES

American Civil Liberties Union
www.aclu.org

Federal Bureau of Investigation Hate Crimes
www.fbi.gov/about-us/investigate/civilrights/hate_crimes

FindLaw (U.S. Supreme Court Cases)
www.findlaw.com/casecode/supreme.html

First Amendment Center
www.firstamendmentcenter.org

Freedom Forum
www.freedomforum.org

Law Library, American Law and Legal Information
http://law.jrank.org

Legal Information Institute, Cornell University Law School
www.law.cornell.edu

National Institute of Justice
http://nij.gov/topics/crime/hate-crime/welcome.htm

Oyez Project, U.S. Supreme Court Multimedia website
www.oyez.org

Supreme Court Historical Society
www.supremecourthistory.org

Supreme Court of the United States
www.supremecourt.gov

BIBLIOGRAPHY

ARTICLES

"About Project Civility." Rutgers University website, http://project civility.rutgers.edu/about-project-civility

Abrams, Floyd. "Right Way to Read 'Hate Speech' Opinion," *New York Times*, July 3, 1992, 24.

"Antonin Scalia." The Oyez Project at IIT Chicago–Kent College of Law, www.oyez.org/justices/antonin_scalia

Bell, Jeannine. "O Say, Can You See: Free Expression by the Light of Fiery Crosses," *Harvard Civil Rights–Civil Liberties Law Review*, vol. 39 (2004).

Block, Melissa. "Comparing Hate Speech Laws in the U.S. and Abroad." National Public Radio, March 3, 2011, www.npr.org/2011/03/03/134239713/France-Isnt-The-Only-Country-To-Prohibit-Hate-Speech

"Campus Environment Team." Arizona State University, https://provost.asu.edu/index.php?q=cet/

Chronis, Peter G. "State Law Expected to Survive," *Denver Post*, June 23, 1992, 1.

Cohen, Adam. "Why New Jersey's Antibullying Law Should Be a Model for Other States," *Time*, September 6, 2011, http://ideas.time.com/2011/09/06/why-new-jerseys-antibullying-law-should-be-a-model-for-other-states/

Cowell, Alan. "A.N.C. Official Convicted of Hate Speech," *New York Times*, September 13, 2011, A8.

Crowley, Andrea L. "R.A.V. v. City of St. Paul: How the Supreme Court Missed the Writing on the Wall," *Boston College Law Review*, 34:4:4 (1993), 790–791.

"David H. Souter." The Oyez Project at IIT Chicago–Kent College of Law, September 22, 2011, http://holmes.oyez.org/justices/david_h_souter

deFiebre, Conrad. "Burning Cross Greets Black Family on St. Paul's East Side," *Star Tribune* [Minneapolis–St. Paul], June 22, 1990, 1.

Editorial. "A Dangerous Precedent," *St. Petersburg* [FL] *Times*, June 24, 1992, 10.

Editorial. "Crossing Free Speech's Line," *Orange County Register* [Santa Ana, CA], June 23, 1992, 10.

Editorial. "Hate Crimes: Court Rightly Identifies Political Correctness Dangers," *Houston Chronicle*, June 23, 1992, 14.

Editorial. "High Court's 'Hate' Decision," *Northwest Florida Daily News*, June 24, 1992, 4A.

Editorial. "Scalia and Pals Give Hatred a Hand," *Buffalo* [NY] *News*, June 29, 1992, B3.

Epstein, Aaron. "High Court Voids Ban on Hate Crimes," *Philadelphia Inquirer*, June 23, 1992, 1.

"Examining the Bias Charge in the Tyler Clementi Case," *Star-Ledger* [NJ], September 11, 2011, http://blog.nj.com/njv_editorial_page/2011/09/examining_the_bias_charge_in_t.html

Federal Bureau of Investigation. "Hate Crime Statistics," 2009, 2010, www2.fbi.gov/ucr/hc2009/incidents.html, www.fbi.gov/about-us/cjis/ucr/hate-crime/2010

Fischer, Norman. "The Moral Core of U.S. Constitutional Bans on Hate Speech Codes," Paideia, Kent State University, www.bu.edu/wcp/Papers/Law/LawFisc.htm

Gendler, Neal. "B'nai B'rith Leader Says Anti-Semitic Acts on Rise," *Star Tribune* [Minneapolis–St. Paul], June 28, 1990, 6.

Greenlaw, Linda. "Even in Agreement, Scalia Puts Roberts to Lash," *New York Times*, June 28, 2007, A1.

————. "High Court Voids Law Singling Out Crimes of Hatred," *New York Times*, June 23, 1992, 1.

————. "Justices to Decide If Hate-Crime Law Illegally Curbs Freedom of Expression," *New York Times*, June 11, 1991, www.nytimes.com/1991/06/11/us/supreme-court-roundup-justices-decide-if-hate-crime-law-illegally-curbs-freedom.html

————. "Justices Uphold Stiffer Sentences for Hate Crimes," *New York Times*, June 12, 1993, http://www.nytimes.com/1993/06/12/us/the-supreme-court-hate-crimes-justices-uphold-stiffer-sentences-for-hate-crimes.html

Gustafson, Paul. "Hate-Crime Ordinance Rejected: St. Paul Measure Limited Free Speech, Court Says," *Star Tribune* [Minneapolis–St. Paul], June 23, 1992, 1.

————. "High Court Will Review St. Paul Hate Crime Law," *Star Tribune* [Minneapolis–St. Paul], June 11, 1991, 1.

————, and Anthony Lonetree. "Judge Tosses Out Part of Cross Burning Ordinance," *Star Tribune* [Minneapolis–St. Paul], July 18, 1990, 1.

Hamburger, Tom. "Hate-Crime Ordinance Rejected: Moves to Fight Bias Crimes Thrown into Doubt by Ruling," *Star Tribune* [Minneapolis–St. Paul], June 23, 1992, 1.

"Hate Crime Laws." Anti-Defamation League, www.adl.org/99 hatecrime/constitutionality.asp

"Hate Speech on Campus." American Civil Liberties Union, www.aclu.org/free-speech/hate-speech-campus

Heman, Ryan. "More Speech, not Less, and Certainly not Hate Speech," *Tufts Daily*, February 15, 2011, www.tuftsdaily.com/op-ed/more-speech-not-less-and-certainly-not-hate-speech-1.2469200?pagereq=1

Hentoff, Nat. "A Startling Triumph for Free Speech," *Village Voice*, July 28, 1992, 18.

————. "This Is the Hour of Danger for the First Amendment," *Village Voice*, January 28, 1992, 21.

Hetter, Katia. "Enforcers of Hate-Crime Laws Wary after High Court Ruling," *Wall Street Journal*, August 13, 1992, 1.

"How Social Media Outlets Impact Digital Terrorism and Hate." Simon Wiesenthal Center, May 13, 2009, www.wiesenthal.com/site/apps/nlnet/content2.aspx?c=lsKWLbPJLnF&b=4441467&ct=6994349

Hudson, David L. Jr. "Hate Speech & Campus Speech Codes." First Amendment Center, www.firstamendmentcenter.com/speech/pubcollege/topic.aspx?topic=campus_speech_codes

Johnson, Kirk, Serge F. Kovaleski, Dan Frosch, and Eric Lipton. "Suspect's Odd Behavior Caused Growing Alarm," *New York Times*, January 10, 2011, A1.

Kane, Eugene. "When Is a Crime Really a 'Hate Crime'?" *Milwaukee* [WI] *Journal Sentinel*, September 8, 2010, www.jsonline.com/news/milwaukee/102499259.html

Lanman, Scott. "Jacobowitz Settles 'Water Buffalo' Lawsuit," *Daily Pennsylvanian*, September 8, 1997, http://thedp.com/index.php/article/1997/09/jacobowitz_settles_water_buffalo_lawsuit

"Legal Limits on Hate Crime to Be Reviewed," *Houston Chronicle*, June 10, 1991, 1.

Lehr, Dick. "High Court Overturns 'Hate Crime' Ordinance," *Boston Globe*, June 23, 1992, 1.

Leo, John. "The Politics of Hate," *U.S. New & World Report*, October 9, 1989.

Lewin, Tamar. "Hate-Crime Law Is Focus of Case on Free Speech," *New York Times*, December 1, 1991, www.nytimes.com/1991/12/01/us/hate-crime-law-is-focus-of-case-on-free-speech.html

Liptak, Adam. "So, Guy Walks Up to the Bar, and Scalia Says . . . ," *New York Times*, December 31, 2005, www.nytimes.com/2005/12/31/politics/31mirth.html

Lithwick, Dahlia. "The Steve and Nino Show," *Slate*, October 6, 2011, www.slate.com/articles/news_and_politics/jurisprudence/2011/10/breyer_and_scalia_unintentionally_make_the_case_for_cameras_in_t.html

Madigan, Michelle. "Internet Hate-Speech Ban Called 'Chilling,'" *PC World*, December 2, 2002, www.pcworld.com/article/107499/internet_hatespeech_ban_called_chilling.html

Malik, Kenan, with Peter Molnar. "More Thoughts on Hate Speech and the Law," *Pandaemonium*, February 15, 2011, http://kenanmalik.wordpress.com/2011/02/15/more-thoughts-on-hate-speech-and-the-law/

Marcus, Ruth. "Supreme Court Overturns Law Barring Hate Crimes," *Washington Post*, June 23, 1992, 1.

Marklein, Mary Beth. "On Campus: Free Speech for You but not for Me?" *USA Today*, November 3, 2003, www.usatoday.com/news/washington/2003-11-02-free-speech-cover_x.htm

Mauro, Tony. "Issue of Cross Burning: A Right? Or a Wrong?" *USA Today*, June 11, 1991, 8.

"New Court Decision Reinforces Need for Speech Policy Changes at Five Colleges, Universities." Alliance Defense Fund press release, August 26, 2010, www.adfmedia.org/News/PRDetail/4315?

"Obama Signs Hate Crimes Bill into Law," CNN, October 28, 2009, http://articles.cnn.com/2009-10-28/politics/hate.crimes_1_crimes-gay-rights-human-rights-campaign?_s=PM:POLITICS

Pankratz, Howard. "Neo-Nazi Gunman in Alan Berg's Murder Dies in Prison," *Denver Post*, August 17, 2010, www.denverpost.com/news/ci_15805243

Pannick, David. "Smother Hate with Freedom of Speech," *Times* [London, UK], July 28, 1992.

Rasmussen Reports. "Americans Still Oppose Ban on Hate Speech." April 28, 2011, www.rasmussenreports.com/public_content/lifestyle/general_lifestyle/april_2011/americans_still_oppose_ban_on_hate_speech

Rowan, Carl T. "Court Encourages Haters and Killers," *Chicago Sun-Times*, June 26, 1992, 35.

Rubin, James H. "Justices Kill Hate Crimes Ordinance," *Morning Call* [Allentown, PA], June 23, 1992, 1.

"Ruling Aimed at Hate-Speech Laws, Scholars Say," *St. Louis Post-Dispatch*, June 24, 1992, 1C.

Savage, David. "Supreme Court Will Decide If It Is Legal to Ban Hate Acts Based on Race, Religion," *Los Angeles Times*, June 11, 1991, 16.

Scalia, Antonin, and Kevin A. Ring. *Scalia Dissents: Writings of the Supreme Court's Wittiest, Most Outspoken Justice*, Washington, DC: Regnery Publishing, 2004.

Schauer, Frederick. "The Exceptional First Amendment." Kennedy School of Government Working Paper No. RWP05-021, February 2005, http://papers.ssrn.com/sol3/papers.cfm?abstract_id=668543

Scheer, Peter. "U.S. Alone in Protecting 'Hate Speech.'" SFGate.com. March 17, 2011. http://articles.sfgate.com/2011-03-17/opinion/28700806_1_hateful-speech-john-galliano-fringe-religious-group

Shively, Michael, and Carrie F. Mulford. "Hate Crime in America: The Debate Continues," *NIJ Journal*, no. 257, June 2007.

"Spotlight on Speech Codes 2011: The State of Free Speech on Our Nation's Campuses." Foundation for Individual Rights in Education, 2011, http://thefire.org/public/pdfs/312bde37d07b913b47b63e275a5713f4.pdf

Starr, Sandy. "Hate Speech: What Is There to Be Worried About?" Presentation to the OSCE conference on Guaranteeing Media Freedom on the Internet, Amsterdam, August 27, 2004, www.osce.org/fom/36098

"The Supreme Court: Wisconsin Court Overturns Stiffer Terms for Hate Crimes," *New York Times*, June 25, 1992, 10.

"3 Boys Convicted of Cross Burning," *Star Tribune* [St. Paul–Minneapolis], February 6, 1993, 2B.

Tsesis, Alexander. "Burning Crosses on Campus: University Hate Speech Codes," *Connecticut Law Review*, 43:2, December 2010, http://rsa.cwrl.utexas.edu/node/4473

Tye, Larry. "Hate Crimes on Rise in US Racial Attacks, Gay Bashing Burgeoning," *Boston Globe*, July 29, 1990, 1.

Uelmen, Gerald. "The Price of Free Speech: Campus Hate Speech Codes," *Issues in Ethics*, 5:2, Summer 1992, www.scu.edu/ethics/publications/iie/v5n2/codes.html

UPI, "3 Muslims Guilty of Anti-Gay Leaflets," United Press International, January 21, 2012, http://www.upi.com/Top_News/World-News/2012/01/21/3-Muslims-guilty-of-anti-gay-leaflets/UPI-27601327123275/

"When Is It Hate Speech?: 7 Significant Canadian Cases," CBC News, October 12, 2011, www.cbc.ca/news/canada/story/2011/10/12/f-free-speech-hate-crimes.html

BOOKS

Cleary, Edward J. *Beyond the Burning Cross*. New York: Vintage Books, 1994.

Collins, Ronald K. L., and Sam Chaltain. *We Must Not Be Afraid to Be Free: Stories of Free Expression in America*, New York: Oxford University Press, 2011.

Gates, Henry Louis Jr., Anthony Griffin, Donald Lively, and Nadine Strossen. *Speaking of Race, Speaking of Sex: Hate Speech, Civil Rights, and Civil Liberties*. New York: New York University Press, 1995.

Jacobs, James B., and Kimberly Potter. *Hate Crimes: Criminal Law & Identity Politics*. New York: Oxford University Press, 1998.

Lewis, Anthony. *Freedom for the Thought That We Hate: A Biography of the First Amendment.* New York: Basic Books, 2007.

O'Brien, David M. *Congress Shall Make No Law: The First Amendment, Unprotected Expression, and the U.S. Supreme Court.* Lanham, MD: Rowman & Littlefield, 2010.

Pohlman, H. L. *Constitutional Debate in Action: Civil Rights & Liberties.* Lanham, MD: Rowman & Littlefield, 2005.

Shiell, Timothy C. *Campus Hate Speech on Trial,* 2nd ed. Lawrence: University Press of Kansas, 2009.

COURT CASES

Apprendi v. New Jersey, 530 U.S. 466 (2000).

Brandenburg v. Ohio, 395 U.S. 444 (1969).

Brockett v. Sokane Arcades Inc., 472 U.S. 491 (1985).

Chaplinsky v. New Hampshire, 315 U.S. 568 (1942).

Collin v. Smith, 439 U.S. 916 (1978).

Doe v. University of Michigan, No. 89-71683, 721 F. Supp. 852 (E.D. Mich. 1989).

In the Matter of the Welfare of R.A.V., Supreme Court of Minnesota, 464 N.W.2d 507 (1991).

McCauley v. University of the Virgin Islands, 618F. 3d 232, U.S. Court of Appeals, 3rd Circuit (2010).

O'Brien v. United States, 391 U.S. 367 (1968).

R.A.V. v. St. Paul, 505 U.S. 377 (1992).

Stanley v. Georgia, 394 U.S. 557 (1969).

Terminiello v. Chicago, 337 U.S. 1 (1949).

Texas v. Johnson, 491 U.S. 397 (1989).

Texas v. Johnson, No. 88-155 (1988), Petitioner's Brief.

Thornhill v. Alabama, 310 U.S. 88 (1940).

United States v. Eichman, 496 U.S. 310 (1990).

United States v. J.H.H., L.M.J., and R.A.V., 22 F.3d 821, 62 USLW 2719, U.S. Court of Appeals, 8th Circuit (1994).

United States v. Morrison, 529 U.S. 598 (2000).

United States v. Schwimmer, 279 U.S. 644 (1929).

United States v. Virginia et al., 518 U.S. 515 (1996).

Virginia v. Black, 538 U.S. 343 (2003).

Wisconsin v. Mitchell, 508 U.S. 476 (1993).

ORDINANCES/LAWS/DOCUMENTS

Additional Protocol to the Convention on Cybercrime, Council of Europe, January 28, 2003, http://conventions.coe.int/Treaty/en/Treaties/html/189.htm

St. Paul Bias-Motivated Crime Ordinance, §292.02 (1990).
U.S. Constitution, Amendment I.
Wisconsin Penalty-Enhancement Law, Wis. Stat. §939.645
   (1991–1992).

WEBSITES

Alliance Defense Fund
www.adfmedia.org

American Center for Law and Justice
http://aclj.org

American Civil Liberties Union
www.aclu.org

Anti-Defamation League
www.adl.org

Bill of Rights Institute
www.billofrightsinstitute.org

FindLaw (U.S. Supreme Court Cases)
www.findlaw.com/casecode/supreme.html
http://supreme.lp.findlaw.com/supreme_court/docket/2003/
   march.html

First Amendment Center
www.firstamendmentcenter.org

Foundation for Individual Rights in Education
http://thefire.org

Freedom Forum
www.freedomforum.org

Law Library, American Law and Legal Information
http://law.jrank.org

The 'Lectric Law Library
www.lectlaw.com

Legal Information Institute, Cornell University Law School
www.law.cornell.edu

National Archives
www.archives.gov

Oyez Project, U.S. Supreme Court Multimedia website
www.oyez.org

Simon Wiesenthal Center
www.wiesenthal.com

Supreme Court Historical Society
www.supremecourthistory.org

Supreme Court of the United States
www.supremecourt.gov

ABOUT THE AUTHOR

Susan Dudley Gold has worked as a reporter for a daily newspaper, managing editor of two statewide business magazines, and freelance editor and writer for several regional publications. She has written more than four dozen books for middle-school and high-school students on a variety of topics.

Her work, which includes series on American history and law, has won numerous awards, including Carter G. Woodson Honor Book, Notable Social Studies Trade Book for Young People, and several first-place awards in the National Federation of Press Women's communications contest. Her most recent books include several titles in the Landmark Legislation series, including *Americans with Disabilities Act* and *Freedom of Information Act*, and the four other books in this series. Gold is the author of a number of books on Maine history.

She and her husband, John Gold, own and operate a web design and publishing business in Maine. They have one son, Samuel; a granddaughter, Callie; and a grandson, Alexander.